W9-BIQ-599

Letting
GO

Letting GO

A Girl's Guide to Breaking FREE of Stress and Anxiety

by Christine Fonseca

PRUFROCK PRESS INC.
WACO, TEXAS

Library of Congress catalog information
currently on file with the publisher.

Copyright ©2017, Prufrock Press Inc.

Edited by Lacy Compton

Cover and layout design by Allegra Denbo

ISBN-13: 978-1-61821-691-5

No part of this book may be reproduced, translated, stored in a retrieval system, or transmitted, in any form or by any means, electronic, mechanical, photocopying, microfilming, recording, or otherwise, without written permission from the publisher.

For more information about our copyright policy or to request reprint permissions, visit http://www.prufrock.com/permissions.

Printed in the United States of America.

At the time of this book's publication, all facts and figures cited are the most current available. All telephone numbers, addresses, and website URLs are accurate and active. All publications, organizations, websites, and other resources exist as described in the book, and all have been verified. The author and Prufrock Press Inc. make no warranty or guarantee concerning the information and materials given out by organizations or content found at websites, and we are not responsible for any changes that occur after this book's publication. If you find an error, please contact Prufrock Press Inc.

Prufrock Press Inc.
P.O. Box 8813
Waco, TX 76714-8813
Phone: (800) 998-2208
Fax: (800) 240-0333
http://www.prufrock.com

TABLE OF CONTENTS

Dedication

Dedicated to my girls, Fabiana and Erika. Remember that stress and anxiety aren't the enemy; they are simply reminders of our need to act on our dreams.

ACKNOWLEDGEMENTS

Writing may appear to be a solitary sport. But as any seasoned author knows, it takes a community to support each and every book that finds its way to a reader. As I finish my 15th book, the reliance on my community to help support my process is no less needed.

To my partner, my husband, my soulmate—thank you for your endless support of this crazy need of mine to express myself in words. You are the reason any of this is possible!

To my amazing children, Fabiana and Erika—from your support as artists, to your support as my kids, you are never far from each and every book. You both provide the inspiration I need to continue what I do each and every day.

To Lacy Compton and the entire Prufrock team—I could not have asked for better partners on this journey. Each new project, each new idea, fulfills me in ways I can't adequately express. Thank you for being my thought partners, my benefactor, and my creative team. You shape my ideas into *more* every single time!

To my coach, my friend, my mentor, Andrea—I am so blessed to have you along this journey. Thanks for the late night e-mails, countless calls, and incredible support. So many projects have been inspired by you and our work!

To my cheerleaders IRL: Jon, Gail, Joelle, Kenny, Mary Beth, Micki, Candy, Regina, Jodi, Corrine, and Stephanie—where do I even begin? Between the titling help, the wordsmith assistance, and the general support, each of you has contributed in some way to this final product. Thank you feels inadequate!

To the young women and parents that bravely shared their stories online, via e-mail, over Skype and Zoom, and in person—your stories of facing your fears and overcoming your battles with stress and anxiety form the basis of everything in this book. More than 500 of you, from five countries, took the time to reach out, participate in focus groups, or somehow share your inner selves with my readers and me. Thank you for forging the path and proving that stress and anxiety are not things to be feared and stigmatized; they are simply things that many of us experience at various times in our lives.

And finally, to each person who picks up this book and reads it—thank you for deciding that you are worth more than the sometimes paralyzing effect of your anxiety. Your fear, your stress, and your anxiety do not define you. These things don't mean you are somehow broken. They are feelings that many humans share and reminders of our need to live in each moment and follow our hearts and dreams.

—*Christine Fonseca*

INTRODUCTION

Stress, worry, anxiety, panic—nearly all of us have felt these emotions at some moment in our lives. For some of us, the feelings come and go as a never-ending tide of emotional context that shapes our life. For others, daily stress escalates to pervasive worry, worry gives way to the avoidance trap of anxiety, and anxiety is punctuated by terrifying moments of panic. The cycle is relentless, leaving us feeling broken.

If the cycle goes uninterrupted, our resilience deteriorates and our brain's ability to integrate information and communicate accurately and efficiently is compromised. Eventually, our quality of life is adversely impacted.

This book was written to change that outcome early in the stress-worry-anxiety-panic cycle. Written as a first level of response, *Letting Go: A Girl's Guide to Breaking Free of Stress and Anxiety* will help you understand the nature of stress and anxiety and the ways your brain can often work against you. Throughout the book, you will learn specific tools and strategies to address the negative impacts of stress and anxiety, as well as to develop a personal roadmap to reframe your stress and anxious thoughts into more productive actions.

About the Book

In 2015, I wrote a book for parents of children dealing with social anxiety, titled *Raising the Shy Child: A Parent's Guide to Social Anxiety*. At that time, I felt pulled to write something for older girls to help them process stress and anxiety and break free from the negative cycle of these emotions. My daughters have struggled with low levels of anxiety, as I have throughout my life. I knew I wanted to support them and others in a way I had not been supported as a young adult; I wanted to provide tools and guidance as they learned to manage everyday stresses and larger anxious feelings on their path toward adulthood. *Letting Go* is the culmination of that wish.

It was conceptualized as a self-help book designed to provide the tools needed to reframe your thinking, employ more effective coping strategies, and build resiliency. Researchers have indicated that this type of self-help method can prove useful in reducing or eliminating the negative outcomes of stress and anxiety (Burns, 2006). Furthermore, independent courses of study have been found to be effective supplements to formalized therapy, providing additional assistance and opportunities to practice between therapy sessions (Kendall & Peterman, 2017).

Letting Go was developed using a cognitive-behavioral therapy model and evidence-based cognitive strategies to help retrain the brain and increase resiliency. Each of the activities, worksheets, and tips was chosen based on evidence of effectiveness in general research or through my personal practice as a school psychologist and life coach.

One last note: This book is not a replacement for therapy or the therapeutic process. This book is meant as a way to independently work through lower levels of stress and anxiety before it becomes all-consuming. It can also be used in conjunction with your mental health professional as a way to improve daily functioning and generalize the principals taught during the therapeutic process. If you find yourself in crisis now or at any time while utilizing this book, please reach out. There are several great national agencies to help, including the Suicide Prevention Lifeline—1-800-273-8255 (available 24 hours a day, 7 days a week), and the National Alliance on Mental Illness (NAMI)—1-800-951-NAMI (6264)—which is available Monday–Friday, 10 a.m.–6 p.m. Eastern time. You can also reach out to your state agencies and local mental health professionals.

How the Book Is Organized

Letting Go is arranged into three main sections covering the biological and psychological impact of stress, anxiety, and panic, and the proactive strategies you can incorporate into your life to lessen the negative consequences of these emotions. The idea is to provide you a complete understanding of both stress and anxiety first, thereby facilitating an understanding of why the proactive strategies are beneficial.

Within each chapter of the book, there are specific strategies for recognizing stress and anxiety, as well as any other concepts presented within the chapter. Additionally, there are specific worksheets to facilitate your understanding of how stress and anxiety impact you individually, as well as strategies to reframe the more negative aspects of each. Completing each chapter are stories from young adult girls, highlighting their paths from being negatively affected by stress and anxiety to finding relief and peace. I've included these stories with the hopes of bringing each concept and strategy into the "real world." The stories, although fictionalized to some degree, were inspired by conversations with more than 500 young women from five countries, as well as stories told to me during my 20 years working with young girls dealing with increasingly high levels of stress and anxiety in their lives. The names have all been changed as well as some of the identifying details. But the points of the stories   the ways stress can impact your life and the strategies that can help—remain the same.

At the end of the book is a selection of resources to extend your study, should you desire more information. These resources, I've found, incorporate the best evidence-based information currently available. Although the list is not exhaustive, I believe you will be able to find what you may need to deepen your understanding of how stress and anxiety may be impacting you, as well as ways to find relief.

How to Use This Book

I designed *Letting Go* for you, a young woman with little or no mental health training. It provides general information about the biological and psychological impact of stress and anxiety on the body and mind. Through the activities in the book, you will gain a deeper understanding of how stress and anxiety affect you directly, both positively and negatively. Additional activities will assist you in bringing your thoughts about stress and anxiety into balance, with the goal of reducing any negative impact.

Start with the early chapters and work through the book in order. Once you've gone through it initially, you are welcome to revisit chapters and activities as needed to deepen your work.

In addition to the activities and stories, each chapter ends with a series of journal questions. Daily journaling is an excellent way to increase your understanding of self and the ways in which stress and anxiety impact you. Spend a few moments each day working through the focus questions I've provided. Write answers without editing your responses. Revisit the answers as needed to gain a clearer understanding of your personal thought processes.

What You May Need

As you've figured out by now, this book was designed to be interactive. There are worksheets, activities, quizzes, and journal prompts for you to use as you discover what your experience with stress and anxiety has been and how to move past the self-limiting and paralyzing thoughts that often accompany these emotions. To complete these tasks, you can use a pencil, some paper, and this book. Of course, if you've checked this book out from your local library, it is important to write on a separate piece of paper and not within the book itself.

There are additional items that can make each activity even better. A journal would be very helpful as you progress through this book. Each chapter includes prompts to assist you in digging deep into the various topics addressed in the book. This can be either a physical journal or something you use online. Additionally, apps and websites including Pinterest, PicCollage, Typorama, or Word Swag can help with some of the visual task suggestions. ThinkUp is a great app for personal affirmations. Other positive psychology recommendations are included in the resource section at the end of the book.

Regardless of how you progress through this book, remember that learning to free yourself from the negative impact of stress and anxiety requires work. The tools provided in this book are meaningless if you don't use them. Commit to trying a few in each section. If one exercise isn't effective, try another. This journey is a personal one. Your path is simply that— *your* path.

Adding Your Voice

This book was inspired by conversations with more than 500 young women and parents from five countries. Through focus groups, interviews, coffee chats, and individual e-mails, girls just like you expressed what it was like to experience high levels of stress and anxiety. They talked about what they felt when stressed or anxious, the strategies that worked and didn't work, and how they learned to change their experiences with stress and anxiety. The wisdom of their words can be found throughout the pages of this book—from the stories at the end of each chapter to the specific strategies recommended.

The stories do not end with these young women. You each have your own understanding of stress and anxiety. And as you work through this book, I am confident that you will find your unique path through the initial feelings and move toward a new expression and a new belief about these emotions. I hope that you will share your wisdom with others, whether through e-mail (christine@christinefonseca.com) or by adding your voice on my Facebook page (@IntenseLifeCoaching).

I invite you to share your truth around stress and anxiety. Your words, your story, can help others find the peace and strength to let go of any negative expressions of these emotions.

A Note to Parents and Caregivers

Some of my most lonely moments came during periods of stress and anxiety. The isolation that sometimes accompanies these feelings functions to maintain a negative experience with stress and anxiety. This is where you can help. It is vital that parents and other role models, mentors, and caregivers support those among us who are stuck in the throes of emotional upheaval. Whether caused by stress, anxiety, or other mental wellness challenges, people struggling to find balance need a network of support that can guide and help.

Parents, in particular, play a critical role. Learning to accept the emotional status of a person without judgment or expectation is very hard at times. But this is exactly what your daughter, niece, student, or friend may need. Take time to read the book alongside the young women in your life. Reflect on the ways stress and anxiety have impacted you. Share your personal stories, including open conversations about the ways you may have struggled and how you managed to find your balance.

As you share your experience, remember that your young adults may have different perspectives. Honor their voice, their path. Guard against projecting your expectations on them, and instead, offer a sense of agency as the young adult women in your life work to find their personal truth, balance, and perspective. Providing a safe harbor of unconditional love is the best way you can help these young women redefine the role stress and anxiety play in their lives.

LIVING IN A STRESS-FILLED WORLD

Girl drama, massive expectations from parents and teachers, the pressure to fit in, worries about the future—sometimes it's all too much. There is plenty to feel stressed and anxious about in today's world. Sometimes you just need to let go of your worries and tap into your inner strength.

Over the next three chapters, you will learn what stress actually is and how it impacts your physical and emotional selves. You will also learn a variety of strategies for managing stress and reframing your thoughts about your emotions.

Before we get too far into this conversation, let's take a minute to evaluate your current levels of stress with Activity 1: My Thoughts About Stress.

It's important that you complete this task before I share my definition of stress. For this exercise, I want you to get very clear on your current beliefs about what stress is, the impact it has in your life, and your current methods of coping when the pressure gets too overwhelming.

After you've completed the brief questionnaire, take a moment to complete Activity 2: Goals for Part I.

Remember to revisit both the questionnaire and the goals worksheet as you move through the rest of the book.

ACTIVITY 1 ⇐
MY THOUGHTS ABOUT STRESS

Directions: Take a moment to read and answer each question. Revisit these questions whenever you want to reassess your thoughts or feelings about stress.

1. What does it mean to be stressed out?

    _____

    _____

    _____

2. Do you consider yourself to be under a lot of stress most days? What things specifically contribute to your stress?

    _____

    _____

    _____

3. Do you think stress is a problem for you? Why? Take a moment to describe how your stress feels.

    _____

    _____

    _____

4. If I had less stress in my life, I would . . . (complete the sentence)

    _____

    _____

    _____

5. What is the worst thing about your stress? What is one thing that would make your stress less of a problem?

    _____

    _____

    _____

ACTIVITY 2

GOALS FOR PART I

Directions: Take a moment to think about why you picked up this book. Set a few goals related to your understanding of stress and the role it has in your life. What do you hope to accomplish as you work through Part I of *Letting Go*?

Goal	Potential Barriers	Action Plan	Benefits to Completing Goal
Example: I want to complete each exercise in the book in order to deepen my understanding of stress and stress management.	◆ *I might not have time.* ◆ *The exercises may confuse me.* ◆ *I might feel stressed as I work through things.*	◆ *I can commit to one or two pages a week.* ◆ *I can reach out to my parents or a school counselor for help.* ◆ *I can use the advice to learn to manage my stress.*	◆ *I will learn how to better manage my stress.*

Chapter 1

STRESS AND ANXIETY:
Understanding the Basics

I woke early, the sun not yet over the horizon. The world looked gray, sleepy, calm. I, on the other hand, was not. In 4 short hours, I would be standing in front of a panel of judges, competing for a spot in the coveted Rose Court. I'd dreamed of being part of the Rose Court in the Pasadena Tournament of Roses Parade since I was a little girl. I'd prepared for this moment for more than 6 years, practicing interviews, learning what the committee would want me to say and do. I knew exactly what to expect. And yet, I was *stressed*.

Like most of the other girls there, I had lived through months of sleepless nights preparing for this moment. I rehearsed every minute of my interview and memorized the way the past members of the Rose Court had acted, the things they had said. There was nothing I hadn't prepared for, no scenario I didn't anticipate. Yet, on the day of competition, I was a mess. My body refused to cooperate with my mind. I felt nauseous to the point of vomiting. My hands and voice shook as I prepared to speak. My mind went blank.

Most of us have felt similar sensations in our lives, either during presentations or competitions, driving to and from school, or handling an emotional situation at home. We've come to call the collections of symptoms *stress*, or maybe even *anxiety*. If the feelings are really extreme, we may even refer to them as *panic*.

Regardless of which word we use, a plethora of negative associations usually accompany these emotions, increasing the stress/anxiety/panic sensations that we experience.

But does it have to be that way?

In this chapter, we will explore the nature of stress and why our bodies and minds react as they do. Specific activities will help you discover your thinking around stress and the role it currently has in your life.

What Is Stress, Really?

Stress—it's an all-too-familiar part of daily life. From a nagging sense of worry to a powerful or overwhelming sensation, stress is a common feeling in our everyday lives. But, what is stress, really?

Definitions of stress vary widely. Some people use the word to refer to the feeling of dread or concern that hits before a test or significant event. Others use the word to indicate anxious feelings or behaviors.

Researchers typically use the term *stress* to refer to a significant emotional experience that involves a mental, physical, and/or behavioral response (American Psychological Association, n.d.). I also like a definition I found on a coaching website, Time Thoughts: "A physical, mental, or emotional response to events that causes bodily or mental tension." (Stress Management, n.d.). In other words, stress is any reaction that causes tension in the body or mind, positive or negative.

Stress is the body's alarm system, alerting us to our need to act. That is why it causes tension. It is neither positive nor negative. It is simply a mechanism our body uses to compel us to respond in some way to a given situation. How we interpret that response, as well as how we interpret stress in general, often determines what impact stress has on our lives.

According to the American Psychological Association (2017), 80% of Americans experience one or more symptoms of stress, including worry, nervousness, headaches, or a sense of being overwhelmed. Based on this statistic, you could say that feeling stressed is part of our collective human experience. Women are more likely to experience feelings of stress over a lifetime. Furthermore, women are likely to develop more significant forms of stress, including anxiety or panic disorders.

Clearly, stress is common. Most of the time, feelings of anxiety abate after the event has passed or some measure of action is taken. If you are stressed about a big test, the feeling often leaves once you start the test. If driving in busy traffic is your source of turmoil, arriving at your destination will typically lessen or eliminate the feeling.

But what happens when the stress doesn't stop after an event has passed? What happens when you live in that state of tension for increasingly longer periods of time? We'll examine that question in Chapter 3. First, I want you to become very clear on what stress is and how our bodies and minds respond. I also want you to begin to identify your personal stress cycle and response. You will need this information as we progress through the book.

Let's start with a little quiz in Activity 3: What's My Stress? This quiz will help you identify typical stress-inducing situations that you may be experiencing.

Revisit this quiz any time you feel like your experience with stress has shifted. It can help you gauge the amount of stress you are under at any given point in time. Although the "amount" is less important than you may think, recognizing when you are under increased pressure will enable you to adjust your thinking or behavior as needed for the situation which is definitely a helpful tool in the long run.

The Brain and Body's Response to Stress

As stated previously, stress is the body's alarm system, compelling you to take action. Much of the time the cause of stress is external: pressures from school, relationship difficulties, overscheduling, and the like. These events can produce a variety of physiological and emotional changes that result in behavioral responses that are adaptive (helpful) or maladaptive (hurtful). Obviously, an adaptive response to stress, one that helps move you back into a state of calm, is the preferred outcome. But how can we help ourselves to consistently respond positively to stress? To answer the question, you must first understand how our bodies respond to stress (don't worry, I promise this won't be like biology class!).

To understand how the brain and body respond to stress, it is important to know how the brain is organized and its primary functions. This is an

ACTIVITY 3 ⮜

WHAT'S MY STRESS?

Directions: Think about your life over the past month. Read each statement and decide if you agree, disagree, or neither agree nor disagree. Circle the appropriate number.

	Strongly Disagree	Disagree	Neither	Agree	Strongly Agree
1. I get upset over little things.	1	2	3	4	5
2. I feel tension in my shoulders, neck, or back.	1	2	3	4	5
3. Breathing is difficult for me.	1	2	3	4	5
4. I experience emotional overload often.	1	2	3	4	5
5. My legs and arms feel weak or shaky.	1	2	3	4	5
6. I am bothered by everyday annoyances.	1	2	3	4	5
7. I yawn often, even when I am well-rested.	1	2	3	4	5
8. I often have sweaty palms, even when I am not exercising.	1	2	3	4	5
9. I often feel scared or afraid.	1	2	3	4	5
10. I experience heart palpitations often.	1	2	3	4	5
11. I feel nervous or worried.	1	2	3	4	5
12. I experience racing thoughts or feel distracted.	1	2	3	4	5
13. I have experienced major changes.	1	2	3	4	5
14. I am more/less happy than I was a month ago.	1	2	3	4	5
15. I am more/less excited about the future than I was a month ago.	1	2	3	4	5

Once you are finished, add up your score. The higher the number, the more intense of a stress response you are exhibiting.

oversimplification of your neurological structures, but you don't need to be a neurologist to understand the basics.

The brain is made up of three global areas, the hindbrain (a.k.a., your "old" brain or "downstairs" brain), the midbrain, and the forebrain (a.k.a., your "new" brain or "upstairs" brain). The limbic system, which handles memory and emotion, is part of the forebrain. However, for this description, I will include the limbic system in my conversations about the midbrain.

The hindbrain handles most of the basic bodily functions that support life, such as eating and breathing. The midbrain operates as a relay station between the forebrain and hindbrain. The amygdala, which is part of the limbic system and located near the midbrain, is involved with emotion, memory, and threat perception. The forebrain is primarily responsible for complex thought, language, logic, and reason. The forebrain provides the internal voice of reason, where the midbrain gives us the emotionally driven inner voice.

When your brain is functioning optimally, there is high integration between all areas of the brain. Right-left hemisphere communication is happening. Vertical communication between the forebrain and midbrain is happening. This integration leads to greater adaptability to environmental stressors.

Consider this typical scenario: A loud alarm blares in the middle of your math class. Immediately, the hindbrain and midbrain initiate a stress response. Your heartbeat increases, adrenaline floods your system, and you are ready to respond. Your forebrain assesses the environment for the threat, engaging your limbic system and your cortex. Information from the environment signals the all clear—there is no immediate danger. Your forebrain tells your midbrain and limbic system to calm. Your heart relaxes and you settle back into your chair and your boring math class.

This is how it works when the brain is well integrated. In Chapter 3, we'll take a look at this same scenario when the communication in your brain fails. For now, let's get back to the biology of stress. In the above scenario, the loud noise of the alarm created stress or tension in your brain and you were compelled to act. Without thinking, your midbrain and hindbrain kicked into gear and initiated a stress response, more commonly referred to as *fight or flight*.

Take a look at Table 1: The Brain and Body on Stress. This is how the human body typically responds during periods of stress. It is the stress response we study in biology class, the one that can lead to adverse health

TABLE 1
The Brain and Body on Stress

The Brain on Stress	The Body on Stress	Fight or Flight
• General feeling of unease • Rapid/mumbled speech • Reduced productivity • Heightened or reduced attention • Emotional upheaval • Irritability • Memory problems • Difficulties learning new information • Confusion • Difficulty making decisions	• Headaches, jaw pain • Grinding teeth • Trembling limbs • Neck, shoulder pain • Blushing, heart palpitations • Cold or sweaty hands and feet • Dry mouth • Difficulty breathing • Changes in appetite and sleep patterns • General fatigue or body aches	• Increased circulation • Increased blood pressure and heartbeat • Tense muscles • Increased oxygen flow • Increased adrenaline flow • Increased sugar metabolization • Decreased digestion • Cool skin/dry mouth • Decreased immune system response • Inhibited reproductive system • Inhibited cognition

concerns if activated too frequently. It is the reason stress is so often characterized as harmful.

As you look through the core features of the fight-or-flight response, I want you to recall your most recent experience with stress. Did you demonstrate any sign of fight or flight? How long did it last? Complete the first section of the checklist in Activity 4: How I React to Stress as you remember your response. Think about several times when you experienced stress to develop a complete picture of how you respond to stress. Beginning to observe your personal reaction to stress will enable you to determine the positive and not-so-positive ways stress currently impacts you.

More Than Fight or Flight

The fight-or-flight response is not the only way your body reacts to stress, it is merely your most common initial reaction, and the one most frequently discussed whenever someone talks about fear. Fight-or-flight is about survival. Every system activated in the brain and body is aroused for one purpose—to outlive the threat. But what if the stress isn't from

ACTIVITY 4 ⇐
HOW I REACT TO STRESS

Part 1

Directions: Check the box for each symptom of a typical stress response you demonstrate.

❏ Need to be alone	❏ Headaches, jaw pain	❏ Tense muscles
❏ Irritability	❏ Grinding teeth	❏ Cool skin/dry mouth
❏ Reduced productivity	❏ Increased feelings of courage	❏ Increased urge to call a friend or talk to my parents
❏ Heightened or reduced attention	❏ Blushing, heart palpitations	❏ Increased excitement or anticipation
❏ Emotional upheaval	❏ Neck, shoulder pain	❏ Trembling limbs
❏ Rapid/mumbled speech	❏ Cold or sweaty hands and feet	❏ Increased urge to take action
❏ Memory problems	❏ Dry mouth	❏ Highly focused attention
❏ Confusion	❏ Difficulty breathing	❏ Urge to help others
❏ Difficulties learning new information	❏ Changes in appetite and sleep patterns	❏ Increased need to be with others
❏ Difficulty making decisions	❏ General fatigue or body aches	❏ General feeling of unease

Part 2

Directions: Using the information from Chapter 1 and the section above, complete the following questions:

1. Which of my typical stress response symptoms are most like a fight-or-flight response? When do these generally occur?

_____

_____

ACTIVITY 4, Continued.

_____

_____

_____

2. Which of my typical stress symptoms are more like a challenge or tend-and-befriend response? When do these generally occur?

_____

_____

_____

_____

_____

3. Are there any patterns to my stress response, times when I am more or less likely to feel stressed out?

_____

_____

_____

_____

_____

4. What is the benefit of knowing more about my stress response?

_____

_____

_____

_____

_____

a life-threatening event? Are there other ways the brain and body can respond? The answer is a resounding yes.

Kelly McGonigal, in her 2015 book *The Upside of Stress*, discussed two additional types of responses, the "challenge" response and the "tend-and-befriend" response. As described by McGonigal, a challenge response occurs when a threat is present, but not life-threatening. Your body energizes as it does with fight-or-flight, but you *feel* differently. Instead of fear, you experience something more like excitement or extreme focus, the way you would after riding a roller coaster or achieving a significant goal. Research indicates that this state often occurs in moments of deep concentration and is linked to what psychologists call a state of "flow" (Csikszentmihalyi, 2008).

Tyna, a young dancer I worked with several years ago, often described the way she felt just before a dance recital in this way. She said she felt "wired" and super-alert. It wasn't like the stress she felt when she was scared or overwhelmed. This response was energizing. It fueled her and enabled her to give a better performance.

I, too, have experienced this type of stress response when I am faced with a tight deadline for a book or before a speaking engagement. I am alert, my heart will pound and I feel *ready*. But unlike the moments when I've been afraid, excitement and happiness follow the stress, not fatigue.

Another stress response McGonigal highlights is "tend-and-befriend." With this reaction, the primary hormone activated is oxytocin. Affectionately referred to as the "cuddle hormone," oxytocin compels us to connect socially. It enables our brain to be more socially aware and rewards us for positive social behavior (Mancini, Littleton, & Grills, 2016). Additionally, this hormone dampens our instinct to flee, bolstering courage (McGonigal, 2015). Have you ever texted a friend after a fight with your significant other or before taking an important test? You were likely experiencing a tend-and-befriend stress response in those moments. Reactions to stress activation vary from person to person. As various biological systems react to stress, our brain stores the information, learning from each experience. The goal, then, is to help the experience be a positive one so that our mind creates a positive stress-response script.

In Chapter 2, you will discover how you can retrain your response to stress, using your thinking skills to better manage stressful situations and reframe the *way* in which you think about stress. For now, I want you to revisit Activity 4: How I React to Stress on page 17, completing the rest of the activity.

Knowing that we have a variety of ways to respond to stressful situations can help us learn to better manage stress. It can also help us learn to change how we view stress in the first place. Tatiana's story highlights how little shifts can have powerful results.

Tatiana's Story

I'm Tatiana, a sophomore attending a small high school in Montana. Like most of my friends, I experience stress—school, problems at home, difficulties with my boyfriend. Sometimes I feel like I can't handle it all.

Most days, the stress is just a little tension along my back or across my chest. I can ignore it and focus on my work. At least, that was what I did in eighth grade. That stopped working for me when I started high school. I can't say what changed. I just wasn't able to ignore the stress anymore. I would sit in my classes (especially history), and my thoughts would race. I could literally feel tension under my skin, tightening my muscles and making it more and more difficult to breathe.

I didn't tell anyone what I was feeling most days. My friends didn't have this problem. I was embarrassed. So I kept swallowing up the feelings and pretending things were fine—that I was fine. Until one day, I wasn't.

I walked to my history class like every other day. Except this time, I thought I was going to pass out. I went to the bathroom, my skin moist from sweat. Something felt wrong—really wrong. My mind raced, and I began to think something was medically wrong with me. Instead of trying to get to class, I went straight to the office. I wanted my mom to come and take me to the doctor.

The health clerk allowed me to call home. No answer. I tried my mom's cell. Again, no answer. The feelings of tightness in my chest increased. A counselor came and spoke to me. With her help, I settled my thoughts. We finally reached my mom, and she came to pick me up.

The urgent care doctor ordered a variety of tests. He said he thought I'd had a panic attack. *It couldn't be stress*, I thought. *I feel like I'm dying.* He suggested I speak with the school counselor again and return to school in the morning. I didn't want to talk to anyone yet.

I went to school the rest of the week, waiting for my test results. The counselor called me into her office. I didn't say much, other than things were fine. They weren't. I was embarrassed by my behavior and afraid of what the test results would say.

Several days passed before my mom got the results. Nothing. I was completely healthy. The doctor again recommended that I speak with the school counselor. I assured my mom that I was fine, and I went back to ignoring my stress.

A month went by and attending class was a struggle. Every morning, I would tell myself the day was going to be great. And every afternoon I would feel like I was going to die, like something was really wrong with me. I remembered what the school counselor and doctor had said about stress, but this didn't really feel like stress. It felt like *more*.

Everything exploded on the day of my semester finals. I went to school like every other day, but the stress was too big to ignore. Sitting in my first class, I felt the room begin to spin. My heartbeat pounded in my ears. I grabbed a pass to the bathroom before I freaked out completely. I texted my mom, telling her I was in the bathroom crying. She told me to go to the office. Before I could get there, she had called them.

The counselor met me at the door. She ushered me into her office quietly and let me cry. Everything came pouring out—the weeks, months, of feeling this way, the way my chest tightened and how I couldn't think anymore.

Ms. Jarvis, the counselor, was kind. She listened to everything I said, scribbling a few notes down on her pad. She asked me about school and home, asked about my experiences with stress. It felt good to speak with her. She gave me a book to read and suggested that I sit in the nurse's office until I was ready to return to class.

Speaking with Ms. Jarvis this one time wasn't a cure for my stress, but it did help. She encouraged me to talk to my parents about everything and to reach out at school whenever I needed.

After speaking with mom, my friends, and Ms. Jarvis, I realized that I was just stressed. Really stressed. I also learned that several of my friends felt the same way. Ms. Jarvis formed a small group with my friends and I. We talked through our stress. This helped so much.

She gave us a few tips for managing the stress, things like mindful breathing and letting go of the stressful feelings. She also taught us to think about stress differently.

As I practiced these exercises, my feelings of stress lessened. The same happened with my friends. The more we talked, encouraged each other, and learned better coping skills, the more we were able to manage our stressful emotions.

Stress is not uncommon in today's world. Everything from the constant pressure to perform on tests at school, to our need to stay connected on social media, to difficulties in our personal relationships—there is no shortage of stressors. Stress can impact your physiology, emotional state, and thinking processes. But experiencing stress doesn't need to overwhelm your coping system to the depth that most of us currently experience. Review the activities found throughout this chapter and begin to learn how you view stress and how this impacts your current life. Then use the journal questions to explore your relationship with stress even more deeply.

Do the Work

As you work through the information within the chapter, pay attention to your thoughts and feelings. Use your journal to process that information and gain a deeper understanding of yourself. The guiding questions below can help. Consider focusing on one or two issues each time you journal.

- How do I define stress? Are there particular kinds of stress that are harder for me to experience than others? Take a moment to think about why these types of stress are more difficult.
- What are my current physical reactions to stress? As I begin to notice my physical reactions more, is my awareness of stress increasing? Why would this be helpful?
- What are my current emotional responses to stress? As I begin to notice my emotional reactions more, is my awareness of stress increasing? Why is this helpful?
- What do I most want to change or develop concerning my experiences with stress?
- What can I do right now to move toward my stress-related goals or desires?

Chapter 2

STRESS IS NOT THE ENEMY

Most of us grew up understanding that stress is the enemy. It's counterintuitive to think of the negative feelings stress brings as somehow being positive. And yet, they can be. At the very least, stress is a neutral event in our lives.

Catalina, a student I worked with, struggled to see stress positively. We first started working together because of school-related performance anxiety. Every time she had a test or a presentation in class, her stomach would do flip-flops and she would feel like she was going to pass out. Sound familiar?

One day, about a month after we had started working together, I asked her to keep track of the positive aspects of stress.

"What positive things?" she asked.

"You know, the ways stress serves you."

Catalina thought I'd lost my mind. How could anything *good* be attributed to stress? Still, I encouraged her to try to view stress in a different way.

Reluctantly, she agreed and started to track anything positive that resulted from stress, no matter how small. Catalina listed things like "I didn't die from the stress," and "The stress went away after the presentation." After a few weeks, the list changed a little, including listings like "I think I'm feeling less stress now" and "Maybe this isn't so bad after all."

Nothing had changed in Catalina's life or her experiences with stress, except the way she started to think about her responses.

In this chapter, we will examine how stress can positively serve your life. We will also explore ways to reframe your thoughts about stress in order to help you capitalize on its more positive aspects.

Stress the Positive

As I mentioned in Chapter 1, there are positive aspects to your stress response. The same hormones that activate your fight-or-flight response in a crisis help you to rise to meet difficult challenges. When these problems aren't life-threatening, your forebrain stays involved, enabling you to make decisions during the periods of stress. The integrated response from your brain creates an adaptive cycle of responding that has the potential to provide courage, compassion, strength, and motivation. I don't know about you, but these all sound like excellent things.

Take a few moments and review Activity 5: The Positive Side of Stress. The positive attributes of our varied stress responses are listed. Review each quality and indicate how each response can have a positive impact on your life. Take a moment to reflect on the stressful moments you've experienced. Think of each moment in detail. Was there a positive side to the event? Did your stress response help you in some way? What are additional positive ways your reactions could benefit you? The more you embrace an adaptive view of stress, the more likely that being stressed will serve as a motivator instead of something to be avoided.

At this point, you may be thinking that all of this talk about the positive side of stress is fine—as long as you aren't already super anxious! It's easy to manage some of the everyday stress that we experience. But what about high levels of pressure, periods of time when it feels as though the world is conspiring against you? It turns out that even during highly stressful times, our response does not have to be toxic. Additional research in the field of positive psychology indicates that even high levels of stress can have a productive and positive impact on general functioning.

ACTIVITY 5 ⇐

THE POSITIVE SIDE OF STRESS

Directions: Consider the following list of positive stress response symptoms. For each one, indicate the potential benefit to you, the probable stress response the symptom is related to, and one situation in which using this response would help you.

Stress Response Symptom	Potential Benefit	Probable Stress Response Used	Additional Ways This Could Be a Benefit
Example: Focused attention	Enables me to figure out what I need to do in the situation	Challenge and fight-or-flight	Enables me to make better decisions in a period of stress
Focused attention			
Increased urge to call a friend			
Increased urge to talk to an adult about a problem or situation			
Increased excitement or anticipation			
Increased courage to act			
Increased desire to take action			
Increased desire to help another person			
Increased need to be with others			

STRESS IS NOT THE ENEMY

Researchers have found that when people are engaged in high levels of activity and indicate elevated levels of pressure, they are also more likely to show a greater sense of fulfillment in their life. Kelly McGonigal (2015) referred to this as the "stress paradox" (p. 64). She went on to say that people who experience higher levels of stress also report higher levels of life satisfaction.

How can this be? Can we train ourselves to view stress in a positive way and change our experiences with stress? I believe we can. It's simply a matter of focusing on the positive aspects of our miraculous stress responses.

In the previous chapter, I asked you to explore your specific responses to stress in Part 2 of Activity 4. You examined when your response more closely resembled fight-or-flight, challenge, and tend-and-befriend. Take a moment to review that exercise (and if you did not complete it, take time to complete it now). In what way are your responses linked to positive outcomes? In other words, how has your stressed served you?

Take a moment to complete Activity 6: How Stress Serves Me. Using the previous checklist of stress response symptoms, think about all of the ways that stress has served you. Stress is truly not the enemy. Learning to shift into a positive view of stress when you feel overwhelmed can make the difference between rising to the new challenge you face and being swept away.

Reprogramming Your Ideas About Stress

By now, you probably have a very clear idea of the role stress has in your life. Perhaps you have negatively viewed stress, becoming overwhelmed by the sheer volume of the everyday expectations you feel. Trust me, this is not unusual. Most of us have too much to do at any given time. Actively shifting how we think about stress, moving from viewing it as overwhelming to seeing the positive aspects, is the key to managing our day-to-day experiences.

One way we can begin to change our thinking is by seeking purpose in what we do. Researchers have found that when we see value in our daily activities, we are less likely to experience those events in a negative way. Furthermore, connecting our deepest personal values with our actions builds our individual capacity for stress (Hill & Turiano, 2014). Each connection we make creates integration in our brains, which leads to more resiliency.

ACTIVITY 6 ⇐
HOW STRESS SERVES ME

Directions: Think about your stress response and answer each question below.

1. How does my fight-or-flight response help me?

_____

_____

_____

_____

2. How does my challenge response help me?

_____

_____

_____

_____

3. How does my tend-and-befriend response help me?

_____

_____

_____

_____

4. How does my body's stress recovery system help me?

_____

_____

_____

_____

Consider the pressure you may feel to do well in school. Driven by both your personal and parental expectations, the odds are good that you feel a lot of stress around academic performance. It's hard to imagine that the pressure is anything other than detrimental to your health. But, what if instead of focusing on the negative feelings of the expectations, you thought about the values of accomplishment and diligence. Instead of focusing on how bad the stress makes you feel, think about the ways you are demonstrating motivation and responsibility when you complete your schoolwork at a high level.

Researchers have found that when you intentionally look for ways to connect your values to your actions, you shift the impact of your stress response from maladaptive to adaptive (Hill & Turiano, 2014). In other words, you switch your stress thinking from negative to positive.

Look at Activity 7: Everyday Values. For Part 1, read each of the listed values and circle those that have the most meaning for you. Your personal values are the things that will drive the decisions in your life. The more your actions are in alignment with your values, the more meaning you find in life.

Part 2 of "Everyday Values" asks you to align your daily activities, the ones that feel mundane or contribute to your stress, with your values. Most of us don't consider the mundane chores of life as having deep meaning for us. But they can. Later in the book, I relay a story about the Quakers. They believed that all actions have the potential for profound meaning when they are in alignment with our values. Your everyday activities can also provide meaning for your life. Training our brains to see the connection between our actions and our values provides meaning that can help us transform our experience with stress.

Once you've completed both parts of the worksheet, think back to a time when you felt overwhelmed with everything on your to-do list. Would your experience with stress have changed if you took a moment to align your to-dos with your values? I believe the answer is yes.

In Part III of the book, I will connect this exercise with an exploration of your personal strengths and a phenomenon called "strengths blindness." Together, these ideas—values and strengths, and their connections to your actions—will give you a blueprint for viewing stress more productively and fusing meaning into your everyday life. For now, practice connecting your values to your actions.

Another way we can embrace a positive view of stress is through empowerment. Empowerment can be described as the act of claiming authority over one's life, or one's actions. During many periods of stress, we perceive

ACTIVITY 7 ⇐
EVERYDAY VALUES

Part 1

Directions: Read each value word. Circle those that best represent your values.

Acceptance	Accomplishment	Adaptability	Adventure	Affectionate
Altruism	Ambition	Appreciation	Approachable	Artistic
Assertiveness	Attractiveness	Balance	Beauty	Belonging
Boldness	Bravery	Calm	Candor	Caring
Charity	Cleanliness	Commitment	Confidence	Conservation
Conviction	Curiosity	Creative	Daring	Dreamer
Depth	Devotion	Diligence	Drive	Education
Empathy	Energy	Entertainment	Enthusiasm	Ethics
Faith	Fame	Family	Fierceness	Fitness
Freedom	Friendliness	Fun	Generous	Gratitude
Happy	Health	Honesty	Honor	Humor
Hope	Humility	Imagination	Influence	Integrity
Intelligence	Intensity	Introspection	Intuition	Involvement
Joy	Justice	Kindness	Knowledge	Leadership
Learning	Logic	Loyalty	Maturity	Mindfulness
Modesty	Motivation	Nature	Neatness	Nonconformity
Open-minded	Organization	Originality	Patience	Passion
Peace	Perfection	Perseverance	Philanthropy	Power
Practicality	Pride	Prosperity	Punctuality	Reasonable
Relaxation	Reflection	Respect	Responsibly	Reverence
Sacrifice	Sacred	Security	Self-compassion	Self-reliance
Simple	Solitude	Spirituality	Stability	Synergy
Teamwork	Temperance	Thoughtfulness	Trust	Uniqueness
Unity	Vision	Vitality	Vigor	Wealth
Wonder	Warmth	Wisdom	Youthfulness	Zeal

Part 2

Directions: List the everyday activities you do, including those that may increase your stress levels. For each activity, choose one of your values linked to that activity.

Activity	Value
Example: Cleaning my room	Cleanliness and organization

a loss of autonomy in our lives. Sometimes this is because we don't have a choice about the activity or situation we are in. Sometimes this is because life just happens. But feeling like we have no choice, or no authority over the situation, contributes negatively to our stress, adding even more anxiety to the situation.

The truth is, we always have some amount of choice within a situation. In my book, *101 Success Secrets for Gifted Kids*, I talk about the Hula Hoop Trick (Fonseca, 2011; see p. 23). In this strategy, you imagine a circle about the size of a hula hoop on the ground. You are in the center of the hula hoop. Everything outside of the hoop, including the feelings, thoughts, and behaviors of others, is outside of your control. Everything inside the hoop—your feelings, thoughts, and actions—is 100% in your control. That is what you can shape, what you can influence. Even in the most difficult of situations, you have some autonomy.

Consider your stress responses in general. You have the power to choose which response you're going to use in any situation. Although there are barriers to this choice at times, it is always possible to change how you respond to any given situation. It is a matter of perspective and practice.

I know—it often doesn't feel like you have a choice as to how you react to situations. There are certain realities you must acknowledge. Perhaps you are living with economic hardship. There may be cultural and environmental factors, things like the community you live in and the options available to you, that also limit some choices. You have rules imposed by parents and school that shape your available options. There are expectations from parents, friends, and the community that influence you. In the end, however, the way in which you deal with those realities, the decisions you make, are yours alone.

In the next exercise, I want you to practice choosing a stress response. For the next week, pay attention to all of your periods of stress, any activity or situation that causes you to feel some amount of emotional tension. Using Activity 8: I Choose, write down the specific event and your initial feeling. Then take a minute to consider your response. Is it better for you to engage fight-or-flight? Or does the challenge response serve you best? Maybe you need to reach out and connect with others as a way to manage the stressful situation. Whatever response you choose, I want you to take a moment and engage. How did you feel? Was the outcome different for you?

I tested out this particular exercise while writing this book. I had been very busy with my day job and other obligations, and had managed to get behind on writing this book. As my book deadline drew near, my stress

ACTIVITY 8

I CHOOSE

Directions: Write down a stressful event you are experiencing. Take a moment to decide which stress response would be the best to use in the situation. Once you indicate which stress response you used, think about why you used it and whether or not it was helpful. Add to this list every time you experience stress over the next week or so.

Stressful Event	Chosen Stress Response(s)	Why I Chose It	Was the Response Helpful? Yes or No
Example: Test in math class	Challenge response	To help me gear up for the test	Yes

levels increased exponentially. Typically, I can positively handle significant amounts of stress. But this time was a little different. My levels of stress were interfering with my ability to complete the book. My feelings of being overcome with anxiety had turned to paralysis. I couldn't seem to write at all. I had to take a look at my stress response and make some changes.

It turns out that I was engaging my fight-or-flight response and looking for ways to escape my stress. This led to less work being done, which increased my stress until eventually I froze. Something had to change.

I utilized some mindfulness activities and chose a new stress response. Instead of engaging fight-or-flight, I needed to engage my challenge response. I needed to use the energy provided by my body and rise to the task at hand. I needed to lean in.

An interesting thing happened—as soon as I shifted my perspective and response, my feelings changed. Instead of feeling stuck or frozen, I felt exhilarated. Leaning in allowed me to find my "flow." I woke each day with new excitement and new determination. Writing the book became a source of joy instead of stress. I was still behind. I still had too much to do. But my experience, my feelings, with the situation had changed. And it had made all the difference.

I'd like to give you one more activity in the area of empowerment. Often people get stuck in the *I can't* mode, seeing only the downside of things. This is normal. Our brains, in an effort to continually keep us safe, see the negative first and foremost. As a result, we overfocus on all of the things we can't do. "I can't write fast enough to finish this essay." "I can't get up in the morning early enough to exercise." "I can't understand this math homework." Statements like these negate anything positive. They take away our ability to move forward and settle us into a fixed mindset.

Shifting into a sense of empowerment involves rewriting this internal dialogue. It means changing the conversation from "I can't" to "I can." The simplest way to do this is through empowering questions. Instead of saying "I can't get up in the morning early enough to exercise," ask yourself "What can I do right now to get more exercise in my life?"

Each time you shift from "I can't" to "how can I," you build a new internal narrative and change your experience with stress. As you move into your own empowerment, you learn that stress is not a strictly negative experience. Each shift in thinking creates new connections in your brain, increasing integration and communication, leading to increased resiliency.

In other words, your ability to cope improves.

Take a moment to complete Activity 9: I've Got This. Each time a stressful situation arises and you find yourself focused on what you cannot do or how the stress is overwhelming you, take a moment to consider what you can do and make the shift.

Embracing Positive Language

Kelly McGonigal's book, *The Upside of Stress*, is built on the foundational belief that how you think about things matters. This hypothesis has been tested and retested, and the results are always the same—our perceptions determine our reality. When you believe that stress helps you, it does. Period.

Pulling meaning from stress-filled events and empowering your autonomy are two good ways to reshape your stress mindset. The next is embracing a positive inner language.

Your mind incessantly engages in self-talk throughout the day, narrating every aspect of your life. In Chapter 4, you will examine the ways your self-talk can help and harm you. For now, I only want you to practice becoming aware of your inner world.

Think about your internal self. What is she like? Does she feel empowered most days? Or is she often scared? Is her voice similar to yours? Or is she younger or older? In the next exercise, I want you to create a persona for your inner self. Describe her as though she were a character in a book, someone different from yourself. Then, answer the questions in Activity 10: The Inner Me.

You may be wondering why I want you to create a persona. The answer is simple. It is easier to observe someone, anyone, other than ourselves. By creating a persona for your inner self, you are detaching from your emotional state, enabling you to objectively look at you. Under the guise of the persona, you can investigate your self-talk, your beliefs, and the inner workings of your mind. By doing this, you will be able to see the positive and negative ways your inner world impacts your outer world.

Over the next several chapters, you will do a variety of exercises to recognize and change errors in your thinking, see the ways your self-talk helps or hurts you, and align your perception with your desired feelings. For now, I just want you to practice observing yourself.

ACTIVITY 9 ⇐

I'VE GOT THIS

Directions: Write down each stressful event. Pay attention to the negative or limiting thoughts you had during the event. Write those in the center column. For each thought, change it to an empowering statement, focusing on what you **can do** instead of things you can't do.

Event	Limiting Thought	Empowering Statement
Example: Audition for community theatre production	I can't do it. I always stumble over my words and freak out. I can't, I can't, I can't. I'll never be good at this. I shouldn't try out. I should stay home.	Auditions are scary. But I really want to be in the production, so I will need to audition. I can practice and be as prepared as possible. After that, I just need to do my best. No matter what happens, I will be okay.

ACTIVITY 10 ⇔
THE INNER ME

Directions: Take a moment and think of your inner persona, the little voice inside your head. Keeping her in mind, answer the interview questions below.

1. Describe your inner persona. What does she look like? Does she have a name? The more clearly you can picture her, the more helpful she will be for you.

_____

_____

_____

_____

2. Ask your inner persona the following questions. Write your answers in the space provided or in your journal.

   ♦ What is your current state of mind? _____

   _____

   ♦ What do you want most right now? _____

   _____

   ♦ What excites you? _____

   _____

   ♦ What scares you most of all? _____

   _____

   ♦ What is your secret wish? _____

   _____

   ♦ What do you love? _____

   _____

Use these questions, and similar ones, to begin to understand your inner self.

Once you've created a persona (you should even give her a name), try observing her everyday functioning. Pick a few random times to watch what she's doing. Jot down your thoughts on the worksheet.

I will refer back to this worksheet periodically throughout the book, so it is important for you to complete this exercise.

Mikayla's Story

Hi! I'm Mikayla, I'm a competitive swimmer, and I know exactly what it's like to be stressed out! When I was 8 years old, I started swimming competitively with a local club team. Day after day I went to practice, determined to learn more, swim harder, be better. My coaches told me that I had great form. They said that if I worked hard, I could get ranked nationally. I believed them.

I competed in my first swim meet 4 months later. It was so much fun. My team and I—we were like a family. Everyone cheered each other on, screaming from the sidelines and encouraging each other just before our events. The crowd was loud. It all felt exhilarating to me.

My coach had signed me up for two events, a 25-meter freestyle and a 50-meter freestyle. I remember what it felt like on the blocks waiting for the race to begin: the way my heart started to pound and my throat began to close. I remember feeling like I was going to pass out at any minute. The feelings only lasted a second or two before the referee blew the whistle and started the race.

The minute I hit the water, everything else drifted away. I didn't notice my pounding heart or my closing throat. All I heard, all I felt, was the excitement of the race. I had found my bliss.

One day, about 4 years after my first swim meet, my coach talked to me about Junior Olympics. She explained that being in JO was a big honor, and with work and dedication I could likely meet the time requirements to compete. It had been my dream to compete at that level, to one day even be in the Olympic games. I asked my coach to push me harder and harder in practice. I begged her to help me meet my time qualifiers.

Finally, I was ready. I entered several swim meets, all with the quest of meeting my time standards for JO. With each meet, the pounding of my heart got louder and louder; my throat closed more and more. And my ability to silence the noise in my head became more and more difficult.

Still I tried each event, determined to make my times. But I wasn't getting faster. Unable to quiet the noises in my head and consumed by an ever-increasing negative voice inside telling me I would never reach my goals, I began to hate swimming.

I missed a couple of practices. I ignored my coaches' suggestions on ways to improve my times. I avoided additional drills, extra opportunities to improve.

My stress continued to grow. Fueled by my current struggles, my brain started viewing the stress as the problem. I blamed my bad times on the stress of school, the pressures of swim practice, and my inability to meet everyone's ridiculous expectations.

The blaming became a self-fulfilling prophecy. The more I talked about the problems of my stress, the worse the stress got. The more I blamed feeling stressed for my inability to improve in the water, the worse my performance became.

Nothing seemed to help. I was ready to give up. After 4 years and 6 months, I was ready to stop swimming completely—the stress just wasn't worth it. I wanted to feel happy again. I wanted a life without the constant feeling of dread every time I got into a pool.

My coach noticed the changes in me, as did my parents. Everyone told me to push past the "fear" they assumed I was feeling. They told me to just swim, the rest would take care of itself.

I tried. I really tried. But their suggestions didn't stop my heart from pounding out of control. Nor did their advice make me excited to swim again. In fact, it seemed the more they tried to encourage me to push past my feelings, the more stressed I became.

I begged my parents to let me stop swimming. They hesitated but agreed to let me quit at the end of the season, as long as I spoke with my coach about everything.

I delayed talking to my coach for as long as I could—it was so hard to admit to her that her faith in me was unfounded. After all, she was the one who thought I would be great. And I was, for a little while.

Finally, I mustered up the courage to tell her I was leaving the team at the end of the season. She asked me to wait to make a decision until after we could talk. A week later, we sat on the pool deck before practice and talked.

"Tell me about what you feel when you swim," Coach said.

I explained about my pounding heart and closing throat. I told her how my mind couldn't focus when I swam anymore. I told her I was miserable.

"What you are describing is one of the ways your body responds to stress," Coach explained. "But there are other ways you respond, too, ways you may not be aware of."

Coach went on to explain that the body is miraculous in how it responds to stressful events. She talked to me about all of the stress hormones and how they fuel the body. And she explained to me how our brains can sometimes react to stress incorrectly, misreading situations as major threats.

Coach asked me to come to practice early throughout the next week so I could learn more about the positive aspects of stress and how my stress could make me a stronger swimmer. She also asked me not to make any decisions until after we'd worked together.

Over the next several weeks, I learned everything I could about stress, our physical and emotional reactions to stress, and how to ensure that we are responding in the most adaptive way possible. I learned that what I think about stress matters. I also learned that I could change what I felt about stress.

I had to work hard to redefine the role of stress in my life. But I did it. I continued to swim. My heart continued to pound before each event, and my throat felt like it was going to close. Now, however, I understood what was really happening—my body was gearing up to meet a challenge. Each heartbeat provided more oxygen to my cells. My throat wasn't constricting, my lungs were drawing deeper breaths in order to best oxygenate my blood. Everything was working in concert to help me do the best I could.

As my ideas about stress began to change, so did my brain's feelings about swimming. The voice in my head started to quiet. I no longer felt damaged or broken. I felt strong.

I eventually did make my JO times. And I recently received a swim scholarship for college. I owe all of this to my coach. She understood that stress wasn't a problem. It was a solution.

STRESS IS NOT THE ENEMY

Stress is not the enemy—this title was selected deliberately. Throughout the last several pages, you've learned how to reframe the way you think about stress. You've learned that stress can be a positive motivator, a call to action, a window into your inner world. More than anything, you've learned that stress, in and of itself, is neutral. It serves a particular purpose in your life.

In the next chapter, we'll talk about what happens when your ability to cope with stress is severely compromised, leading to more anxious responses. Until then, take a moment to work through the reflection questions below. These questions can help you identify the positive role stress can take in your life.

Do the Work

Continue to pay attention to your thoughts and feelings throughout this chapter. Use your journal and the reflection questions below to help:

- In what ways does my stress serve me?
- What mindset around stress is the most difficult for me to change? What would happen if I let go of that difficulty and the negative mindset?
- In what way do I positively refer to stress currently?
- Which stress responses do I most frequently use? Is the response helpful or not helpful?
- What can I do right now to move toward my stress-related goals or desires?

Chapter 3

WHEN ANXIETY TAKES OVER

Becoming good at stress, as Kelly McGonigal (2015) would say, does not inoculate you completely from experiencing anxiety. Understanding the positive role stress can play in your life and shifting your thinking to view stress as adaptive doesn't guarantee you won't get overwhelmed. The truth is, you likely will. Relationship struggles, problems at home, a car accident, or even a significant natural disaster can easily derail anyone. This does not mean you will automatically struggle with anxiety over the long haul.

That said, many individuals do deal with persistent stress that overwhelms their ability to cope. When this condition occurs with increasing frequency and begins to significantly impact daily functioning, then it's time to consider an anxiety disorder.

This chapter focuses on both low-level, everyday anxiety and the escalation to something more significant. The activities are designed to help you understand the way anxious feelings may be impacting you and assist you if you begin to suspect an anxiety disorder. Throughout the sections, you will learn about the physical and biological aspects of anxiety, as well as some ways to mitigate the adverse impact of significant anxiety.

It is important to note the distinction I am making between stress and anxiety. For the purposes of this book, I refer to stress as the warning sign that something needs to be addressed. Anxiety is more. It is the deluge of negative thoughts and emotions paired with the failure of coping strategies that occurs in periods of significant or unexpected stress. I make this distinction as a matter of clarity. Many books on the topic of stress and anxiety use the words interchangeably. Unfortunately, I believe this has led to a tendency to overdiagnose anxiety disorders and downplay the normal functioning of stress, anxiety, and our stress responses in everyday life.

When Stress Becomes Something More

We've all felt it from time to time, that moment when the pressure becomes too much to handle. Our heart pounds too fast in our chest. Our throat constricts and we feel like we can't breathe. Feelings of fear, anxiety, sadness, anger, or depression flood our system. We panic. Trapped in the throes of our emotions, we are unable to think. It feels like our forebrain took a vacation. In fact, maybe it did.

Significant levels of stress cause our body to slam into full fight-or-flight mode. Our adrenal gland pumps out cortisol and adrenaline. Any benefit from our oxytocin response is overridden by the emotions of sadness, anger, and fear. Instead of reaching out, we flee. Or, if we do reach out, we bombard our relationships with the intensity of our emotions, resulting in a negative exchange.

What is happening? Why isn't our forebrain being rational?

The answer lies in our biology. In Chapter 1, we talked about the dance between our forebrain and our midbrain. When the communication works, when our brain is well-integrated, our stress response is typically adaptive. However, when our coping system is compromised due to an overwhelming situation or chronic toxic levels of stress, the communication between the regions of our brain is compromised. Our body goes into survival mode.

This is the biological nature of anxiety.

Anxiety impacts your body and mind on every level. It varies in intensity and duration from person to person, and situation to situation. It can be tied to a particular situation or event, or be spontaneous. Anxiety can even occur in response to the anticipation of an event. Often characterized as an emotion born of avoidance, anxiety can intensify or increase the more you try to avoid it.

Symptoms of anxiety mirror the fight-or-flight response, including heart palpitations, headaches, and feelings of distress (see Table 2). In its more extreme forms, anxiety symptoms can include numbness, dizziness, compromised internal temperature regulation, and increased fear responses. Most of these symptoms occur as a result of the biological changes that occur during your stress response.

In addition to the physical symptoms of anxiety, your thoughts shift as well. Increased negative self-talk, threat perception, and errors in thinking are consistent with high levels of anxiety. As your thoughts change, your feelings shift to more negative emotions. Fear, sadness, and aggression take center stage.

If your thoughts and feelings shift, so do your behaviors. Increased avoidance and nervous behaviors are typical during extended periods of anxiety. The cycle is self-perpetuating, as your actions validate your fear thoughts, and your thoughts increase your feelings, which generate additional behaviors.

This pattern of behavior demonstrates the underlying problem of anxiety—habituation. When anxiety is avoided, the cycle perpetuates, and our response becomes habit forming. Every time we engage in the behavior, every time the cycle continues, we teach the brain that stress is bad, anxiety is to be avoided, and our survival depends on that avoidance.

To see how this plays out for you personally, I want you to remember a time when you felt really, really anxious in Activity 11: Me and My Anxiety. Be sure to complete each section of the worksheet.

What were you thinking during the anxiety attack? How did you feel? Did your thoughts, feelings, and emotions cycle? Understanding your current experiences with anxiety will help you as you move from avoidance to release.

The Brain on Anxiety

This book is not meant to dive deeply into human anatomy and neurology. But you should have a basic understanding of how the brain functions when it is confronted with significant anxiety. Just as before, I will be speaking in generalities. Our actual neurological functioning is somewhat more

TABLE 2
Anxiety Symptoms

Below are the typical symptoms of anxiety. You will notice that they resemble the symptoms of stress. That is because both involve your fight-or-flight response. Think of anxiety as stress amplified.

• Restlessness	• Fatigue	• Avoidance behaviors
• Sleep and/or eating problems	• Stomachaches/ headaches	• Fight-or-flight responses
• Irritability	• Muscle tension	
• Worry or unease	• Poor concentration	

complicated than it may seem as I describe it. But you do not need a Ph.D. in neurological science in order to reshape your experiences with anxiety.

As discussed in Chapter 1, active communication between the forebrain and the midbrain is required in order to balance emotional responses and build resiliency. When our brain becomes overwhelmed with intense emotions, as is the case with anxiety, our amygdala and other fear centers of the brain are activated. When the amygdala is busy talking, the prefrontal cortex—the part of your brain making rational decisions—is silent.

Let's think about that for a moment. If our prefrontal cortex is silent, we are not analyzing the context of emotion. Nor are we discerning the validity of our thoughts or our perceived threats. In the example given in Chapter 1 of the alarm sounding off during our math class, instead of taking a moment to process the *threat* of the alarm, we would only act on that threat. We would likely run from the room, believing our lives were in danger. This is because the primary job of the amygdala and fear centers is to keep us safe.

This activation of the amygdala and shutting down of the prefrontal cortex makes sense when we are in life-threatening situations. If we are being threatened by a large black bear, it does not help us to wonder about how the bear's fur feels or whether or not the teeth feel sharp. No. We need to just act (by escaping or engaging) and survive. The problem comes when this response occurs outside of a life-threatening event.

With anxiety, that is precisely what often happens; we respond to events as though our lives are in danger, regardless of the truth.

ME AND MY ANXIETY

Directions: Think about a time when you felt anxious and complete the grid below.

When I am anxious, my thoughts are . . .	When I am anxious, my feelings are . . .
When I am anxious, my behaviors are . . .	When I am anxious, my body feels . . .

Trauma and Toxic Stress

Adverse Childhood Experiences, or ACEs, are common. Things like divorce, physical and emotional abuse, neglect, and medical/mental health challenges in families can result in trauma within the household. When the trauma caused by these events is pervasive or reoccurring, complex trauma and toxic stress are often the result.

Unlike your typical stress response, toxic stress can have a significant negative impact on your health and well-being. Children and teens who've been exposed to significant trauma and toxic stress are at higher risk for:

- alcohol and substance abuse,
- heart problems,
- anxiety/depression,
- obesity,
- chronic obstructive pulmonary disease (COPD),
- sexually transmitted infections and diseases,
- cancer,
- liver disease,
- negative health outcomes, and
- violence.

Toxic stress occurs when the stress response moves from adaptive, or something that helps us cope with the events, to maladaptive, or something that prevents us from responding in a healthy way, as the mind and body prepare for pervasive and unending threat. When this happens, the brain tells the body to conserve all energy. Any form of change, internal or external, is considered threatening. Your brain locks up and refuses to learn anything new, whether that means learning at school or learning new coping skills. This significantly compromises recovery, as the mind and body work together to resist any and all growth. Toxic stress negatively impacts brain development, bodily functions, memory, learning, emotional regulation, behavior regulation, and social development.

If you are experiencing toxic levels of stress related to ACEs, please reach out to a mental health professional. You can recover from toxic stress, but you must take action.

As our bodies respond without the benefit of our prefrontal cortex, we develop a script for what threat and fear mean in our lives. The fight-or-flight response habituates and our fear narrative, the internal "story" of what fear means in our lives, solidifies. To make matters worse, our body's natural post-stress recovery process typically involves a mental debriefing of the events. As our amygdala quiets and our prefrontal cortex comes back online, we internally analyze past events. Because the communication between the forebrain and midbrain was compromised, we have an incomplete picture of what occurred. Thoughts and emotions driven by our amygdala and fear narrative fill in the missing pieces, painting a picture of increased threat. Part of us knows the picture is incomplete or inaccurate, so we relive the events over and over, attempting to find the errors. However, each time we relive the events, our thoughts confirm their accuracy and increase our feelings of anxiety. Eventually, we become convinced that the fear narrative is *truth*.

This is how *cognition errors*, or mistakes in your thinking, occur.

Let me give you an example. A middle school student I once worked with was terrified being left alone. When she was 5, she took a trip to visit her father alone. Although the airplane staff knew she was traveling alone, the girl did not know she was supposed to wait to disembark the plane when it landed. She got up and walked off the plane without an escort. The girl had never met her father before (he left when she was a baby), so she did not know what he looked like. She waited at the airport for a very long time before she finally connected with her father. Needless to say, this was a scary event for her. Although nothing "bad" happened to her, she had a strong emotional reaction and her brain learned that being alone can be danger-ous. A few years later, she was dropped off at school too early (her mom had forgotten the time change). No one was there and she felt abandoned . . . again. Once again, her brain learned that being left alone was threatening. Any time she got lost in a store or felt abandoned (even if she wasn't), she would experience anxiety and her belief that being alone equaled danger would strengthen.

In truth, it can be dangerous to be left alone at a store or airport. Or to be left alone at home. But the girl overlearned the threat. As she analyzed the events over and over, she began to believe that *every* time her parent was not with her, including when she was at school or with another care-giver, she was in danger. This idea had become her "fear narrative" or her story of fear.

I want you to take a moment to examine your thoughts and discover your story of fear. Using the persona you created for your inner self in Chapter 2, imagine times in which she was afraid. What was happening? How did she respond? What were her thoughts after the event? How did this begin to form her inner story of fear? Complete Activity 12: Thinking About My Fear from the perspective of your inner persona.

As your ability to observe the connection between your thoughts, feelings, and behavior improves, you will begin to see the role of anxiety in your thinking. We will explore more about our fear narratives in Chapter 9, including more ways to recognize and correct inaccurate fear stories.

Learning to Lean In

As I mentioned earlier, anxiety is often defined as a problem of avoidance. As the cycle of increased stress and worry flows, our desire to avoid the negative physical and mental sensations fuels our anxiety (see Figure 1).

Let me explain: It is okay to want to avoid a scary or uncomfortable situation. Most of us have felt that way at some point. However, researchers have discovered that each time you avoid stressful or anxious situations, you actually create greater levels of stress and anxiety (Liu, 2013). Rather than prevent increased stress, avoidance creates less tolerance for anxiety and adversity. Breaking free from the negative impact of anxiety must then involve learning to lean into anxiety, to give into your feelings at the moment without resistance.

Scary thought, isn't it? In fact, it may even seem counterintuitive. But facing your anxiety, and learning to increase your tolerance for adversity, will change your personal experience with both.

You will explore many ways to lean into anxiety and fear over the next several chapters. For now, I want you to strengthen your ability to observe yourself during fear. Using your journal or Activity 13: A Moment in Fear, write about a time when you were highly anxious or afraid from the perspective of your inner persona. Describe each moment in detail. If you struggle to remember, just write what you can. Your ability to objectively describe your fear and anxiety will improve with practice.

I encourage you to repeat this exercise several times over the next few weeks. Each time you experience a moment of anxiety or fear, describe the events, your thoughts, and how you felt. Always use your inner persona's

ACTIVITY 12 ⬱

THINKING ABOUT MY FEAR

Directions: Think about your inner persona, the one you created for the "Inner Me" worksheet. Ask her the following questions. Write your answers in the space provided or in your journal.

- What frightens you or triggers your fear? _____

  _____

  _____

- When you are afraid, how do you act? _____

  _____

  _____

- When you are afraid, what do you feel? _____

  _____

  _____

- When you are afraid, what do you think about? _____

  _____

  _____

Take a moment to think about the different times you've felt fear. What is your "story of fear"? How has it shaped you? Using the perspective of your inner persona, write down that story.

_____

_____

_____

_____

_____

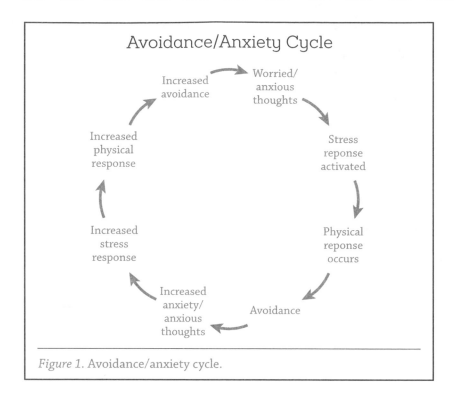

Figure 1. Avoidance/anxiety cycle.

perspective or point of view. This will enable you to detach enough to objectively witness yourself.

In Part II of this book, you will learn specific strategies to correct any thinking errors or change your responses to this type of event.

Izzy's Story

Thanks for taking the time to share your experience with anxiety today. I thought I'd start by asking how it all started? When did you first realize you were experiencing anxiety?

IZZY: I'm not sure I remember a time without it, actually. Well, that's not completely true. I do remember some things—like feeling like I was going to pass out in the middle of my math class, or the sensation of the walls closing in every time I was called on in English. And I remember struggling to come to school at all. That one started in middle school. Mostly, my anxiety just started to happen. It began

ACTIVITY 13 ⇐

A MOMENT IN FEAR

Directions: Take a moment and think about a time when you were afraid. Write a story about the event. Remember to include a description of the event (who was with you, what you were doing), how you felt, and what you were thinking. Use the perspective of your inner persona to write your story below.

One day, I was very afraid. I _____

_____

_____

_____

_____

_____

_____

_____

_____

_____

_____

_____

_____

_____

_____

_____

_____

_____

_____

_____

_____

with a feeling that I was choking. My head would pound, my pulse would race, and I would feel like the whole world was crashing around me. Every instinct told me to run, hide. But there was nowhere to run. No place to hide. The feeling never really went away. These moments lasted a short time and were pretty rare initially. But over the course of a few years, they increased. Just before I got help, I felt these feelings multiple times a day.

You mentioned that things seemed to start in middle school. Do you remember a specific event or trigger? Or did you just start feeling that way?

IZZY: I've always felt a lot of stress. Things were often hard at my house. My parents fought a lot until they finally divorced when I was 9. I lived with my mom after that. We never had a lot of money. She was never really around. I was used to feeling stressed out. But it wasn't until seventh grade that I became completely overwhelmed by it all.

You mentioned that your feelings of being overwhelmed increased over the next few years. Did you try to get them to subside at all? Or seek outside help?

IZZY: Oh yes. I talked with my mom and the school counselor about everything when it first happened. My mom suggested that I try to ignore the negative self-talk. She told me to smile more, go out with my friends, and enjoy life. She said life would be hard soon enough; there was nothing for me to stress over yet. I did what she said, but it didn't help. As I ignored the anxious feelings, they seemed to get worse.

My school counselor suggested something a little different. He said that my brain was overresponding to the environment. He suggested that I ignore the messages of my mind and tell myself to relax. He taught me how to breathe when I was stressed. And he told me to make sure I got enough rest. I tried to follow his advice, too. Like before, things got worse. The more I ignored the negative, scary thoughts running through my head, the more the thoughts would come. I tried the deep breathing and I tried to be more balanced. But it got harder and harder for me to sleep. And nothing seemed to relax me.

I finally gave up on all of the help. I didn't want to disappoint my mom or the counselor, so I just pretended everything was okay. I went to school, often hiding in the bathroom or asking to go to the nurse. My grades were good, but it was a struggle keeping them that way. I pushed through everything. It worked for a little while.

Eventually, though, it all became too much.

When did everything become "too much?"

IZZY: In high school. The extra demands from the teachers, not to mention social pressures—I couldn't handle it all. I started skipping school. I just couldn't manage everything. By the end of sophomore year, I was barely attending. Mom got calls daily that I had skipped school. She was frustrated and didn't know what to do. She took me to therapists, doctors, even a weeklong camp for kids with anxiety. Each thing worked for a few weeks. Nothing worked for long. It was so hard to follow the advice I was given. Meds helped sometimes, but even with that I couldn't seem to manage my anxiety. It was a tough time for me.

What finally helped you?

IZZY: Honestly, I think some of it was maturity. That had to come first. The rest was looking at the whole story of who I am, what I've experienced in life. The last counselor my mom found had a way of helping me see the connection between my parents' divorce and all of the fighting in the house and my stress response. She helped me realize that swallowing my fear was a survival technique I'd learned early on. It served me well for a long time. But it also made my brain hypersensitive to emotions. It was the hypersensitivity that was causing a lot of the anxious behaviors.

Don't get me wrong, I don't blame my parents or my childhood for anything. I mean, stuff happens, right? It was just a difficult situation. But the way my brain interpreted it caused me difficulties later in life. I had to learn how to retrain my thinking. Once I got a handle on that, I was able to heal and move forward.

Izzy's story does not end there. She has consistently been involved in her current course of therapy for a few years. Over that time, she has significantly reduced her anxious responses to life. She is stronger and more capable of managing the stressors of life and is currently finishing her degree.

When stress grows and becomes completely overwhelming to your mind and body, anxiety will likely form. The brain's ability to integrate the information coming in through your senses, your thoughts, and your feelings can become compromised, resulting in increased anxious responses to a variety of situations. Even events that have never elicited a significant stressful response now have the potential to overwhelm you. It is important to gain a handle on both your reactions and your thinking about that response at this juncture, before maladaptive strategies become habituated.

In the next section, you'll learn about anxiety and panic in more detail. You'll also complete activities designed to help you develop the tools needed to break free from an anxious response cycle. For now, take a moment and reflect on how stress has magnified into something more in your life. Answer the following reflection questions to gain the insight needed for the next section of the book.

Do the Work

Use these questions to guide your reflection on the information within the chapter and your thoughts and feelings. Consider focusing on one or two issues every time you journal.

- Are there times when my stress grows into an anxiety attack? If so, when does this happen and why do I think it occurs?
- What are the mental messages I say during periods of anxiety? How can I rewrite them?
- Where does anxiety live in my physical body? What does it feel like?
- What images come to mind during periods of anxiety? Are there colors that align with these pictures? What meaning can I discover from these things?
- What can I do right now to reframe my current experience with heightened stress and anxiety?

MANAGING ANXIETY

As you learned in the previous section, sometimes stress becomes too overwhelming to the nervous system and brain, causing our bodies to react in a hypersensitive way to perceptions of threat or harm. We call this *anxiety*, an *anxiety attack*, or *panic*. The physical sensations of anxiety can often be extreme, mimicking severe gastrointestinal problems, auto-immune reactions, and heart attacks. Over time, toxic stress may even cause the same physical conditions.

As scary as all of that is, toxic stress and anxiety can be managed. We learned a few strategies in the previous section. This next part is dedicated to a variety of methods and strategies for managing and releasing anxiety and panic. It starts with a stronger understanding of the brain's role in anxiety. From there, we'll develop a deeper understanding of our response to anxiety, the mental messages influencing that reaction, and ways to rewrite the messages that no longer serve us. Finally, we'll talk about one of the most extreme versions of anxiety—panic attacks. We'll dive into the science of a panic attack and how to move out of the terror-filled moments into a state of calm.

Just as we started the previous section with a questionnaire, I'd like you to revisit the self-reflection exercise, Activity 11: Me and My Anxiety from Chapter 3 (p. 45). Do you need to add anything? If so, update the worksheet.

Once you are finished, take a moment to think about what you'd like to accomplish in this section and complete Activity 14: Goals for Part II.

Remember to revisit both the reflection exercise and the goal worksheet as you move through the rest of the book.

ACTIVITY 14 ⇐

GOALS FOR PART II

Directions: Take a moment to think about the next section of the book. Set a few goals related to anxiety and panic and how you manage them. What do you hope to accomplish as you work through Part II of *Letting Go*?

Goal	Potential Barriers	Action Plan	Benefits to Completing Goal
Goal: Practice ways to think about my anxiety differently and better understand my fear narrative.	I might decide not to read the book. I won't do the exercises. I might make excuses as to why the exercises don't really work.	I can commit to reading for 5 minutes every night. I can commit to trying each activity. I can try to see the positive in what I am doing.	I will be able to work through my anxiety and have less anxious moments. I will better understand how to reframe my thinking.
Goal:			
Goal:			

Chapter 4

INVISIBLE MONSTERS

I often think about anxiety as producing monsters in my mind. This stems from a few reoccurring dreams I had as a child. The dreams typically came in reaction to significant stress and anxiety. They always started the same: I would start off feeling good, then a horrible sense of dread would suddenly coat my thoughts, forcing me to run. I'd run and run through the caverns of the dream, desperate to escape . . . something. I knew a monster of some form was after me, waiting for me to trip or fall. In the dream, I ran fast, hid well. The monsters, who were always invisible, never found me. But with each dream, I was afraid they would.

I was well into my adulthood before I understood the dreams fully. I began to recognize the signs of anxiety woven throughout the dreams, label my internal thoughts, and read my fear narrative. These were my first steps on my road to releasing the hold anxiety had on my life.

Over the next several pages, you will learn about the monsters in your mind. You'll examine how your thoughts help and when they hurt. You'll begin to identify the subtle ways your brain cons you into believing your fear narrative, and you'll start to determine the things that most typically trigger you (mine usually involved too many commitments, too many expectations, and too little sleep).

The Monsters in Your Mind

All of us engage in self-talk, the constant narration of our lives. Thoughts cycle, providing feedback on everything from our environment to our internal ramblings. Some of this self-talk is important, guiding us toward the direction of our deepest desires, passions, and purpose. Much of our self-talk, however, is not. The ramblings of our mind translate our internal story into short clips, taglines about our "self." All of the chatter is set within the personal context of perspective. If our point of view is positive, we will likely have positive internal messages. Likewise, if our internal view is negative, our thoughts will be negative.

Have you ever taken the time to listen to these ramblings? You might be surprised if you did. Think of the last time you made a mistake in class. What did you tell yourself? Were you encouraging? ("I can't worry, I'll do better next time.") I doubt it. More than likely you said something along the lines of "That was stupid! I should have studied more." Or maybe your personal narrative was more like "Mom said if I didn't study, I wouldn't do as well. I guess she was right." Or maybe even "I'm too dumb to learn this. Why am I bothering?" Regardless of the way you talk to yourself, odds are really good that you engage in some form of negative self-talk throughout the day.

Self-talk doesn't only occur in response to our environment. Often our internal narrative drives our reality. Let's say you have a fear of public speaking. You may imagine yourself choking on stage, unable to speak. You hear people beginning to laugh at you, leaving you humiliated. As the mental story plays out in your mind, you start to feel emotions based on your thoughts. Fear and worry trigger increased negative thoughts, which in turn create more fear and worry. The cycle continues on and on. You tell yourself you are in danger. You *feel* like you are. You begin to believe the internal dialogue, regardless of whether or not it's true. The cycle progresses. Your monsters are born.

Distinguishing between appropriate fear and toxic levels of anxiety is important. Appropriate fear occurs when we *are* in actual danger. Our thoughts warn of an impending threat. Fear centers are activated and our fight-or-flight response mechanism begins. This is appropriate. There is a significant threat that needs our attention.

But what happens when our thoughts are wrong, when we distort reality? This can occur for a variety of reasons. Maybe we have lived in a significant state of anxiety and stress for so long that our threat perception mechanisms have become overly sensitive. Maybe we've experienced trauma that has changed our internal messages and fear narrative.

Physiological, environmental, and emotional dynamics can all influence how we respond to stressful situations. When an anxious response habituates, or becomes our dominant way of responding to stressful events, we may need to re-evaluate how we are functioning.

Self-talk, distorted reality thinking, intense feelings, poor tolerance for stressful events, and masked emotions can all lead to an influx of mental monsters. Fortunately, understanding how each of these things contribute to anxious response patterns and learning what you can do to mediate each of these areas, will help you slay the beasts in your mind.

I want you to think about a time when you felt high levels of anxiety. Using Activity 15: Witnessing, write about the event or situation.

What happened? What were you thinking about at the time? How were you feeling? What actions did you take? By evaluating each of these aspects of the event, you are beginning to see your thought ⤞ feeling ⤞ behavior cycle. This strategy will enable you to turn your lens inward and evaluate some of the inner workings of your mind. This is the first crucial step in becoming aware of your anxiety and how it impacts you. You may want to use your persona developed in the previous section to assist with this process.

Repeat the activity a few times over the next several days. The idea is to increase your awareness of your anxiety chain, strengthening your ability to witness your internal narratives.

After you've had some practice recognizing the connections between your thoughts, feelings, and actions, I want you to begin to chronicle your daily self-talk with Activity 16: A Day in the Life . . .

Pick a random period of the day, alternating the time on each occurrence. For 10 minutes, pay attention to your internal thoughts. What are you thinking about? What are you saying to yourself? Write everything down. Be careful not to pass judgment on yourself during this task. The only purpose of this work is to grow your awareness of your self-talk. Repeat this exercise at least five times. What did you notice overall? Were there any spe-

ACTIVITY 15 ≤

WITNESSING

Directions: Think about a time when you experienced high levels of anxiety. Complete this worksheet indicating the event, your thoughts, your feelings, and your behavior. Use this tool to assist you as you try to change your thinking patterns.

Description of Event	Thoughts at the Time of the Event	Feelings During the Event	Behavior During the Event
Example: Eating dinner with friends.	Oh no, what if I get sick when I eat? Maybe I shouldn't eat anything at all.	Fear, worry, nervousness, tension, upset stomach.	Avoidance of the event. Going to the bathroom just in case I need to vomit.

After you've completed the worksheet with a few events, review your responses. Are there any errors in your thinking? Combine this activity with Activity 22: Prove It! (p. 82) to help you correct cognition errors.

ACTIVITY 16 ⇐

A DAY IN THE LIFE . . .

Directions: Pick a random date and time. Observe your inner thoughts and feelings for 10 minutes. Write down every thought during this time. At the end of the time period, write down the feelings you noticed. Repeat this activity on several different dates/times over the next few *weeks*.

Day/Time	Thoughts	Feelings
Example: Monday, 11:30 a.m.	I'm stupid. Why am I doing this task? This book is dumb. I'm dumb. Look, a bird. That's cool. Why am I doing this again? There are so many cars outside. I like white cars. Why are there so many people out? My neck hurts. I think I'm hungry. It's really hard keeping track of my thoughts. Yep, I feel dumb.	Boredom, anxiety/stress, frustration, annoyance, nothing

After you've written a few time samples down, take a moment to review what you wrote. Do you notice any patterns? Any themes? Are there things about your ramblings you think are important? Things you want to continue or change?

cific patterns that developed? Engage in this activity a few times through-out this book to gain perspective and adjust any distortions of thinking.

As you become aware of your cognition errors and negative self-talk, you will begin to notice how your internal monsters keep you trapped. In the next section, we will explore how the brain cons you into believing your worst thoughts.

The Seven Cons

Our brains are wonderful things, capable of creating our wildest dreams and our scariest nightmares. Making decisions in mere nanoseconds, our brains are incessantly busy sending and receiving messages, often without any conscious effort on our parts. Whether we are aware of our internal chatter or not, one thing is certain: Our brains work tirelessly to kept us safe. But it isn't just things out in the world that our brains protect us from, they protect us from our internal monsters as well. And these are often perceived as more threatening than anything outside of the body.

Human beings hate change. At our most primal and cellular level, our minds work to maintain a specific homeostatic state. When something, anything, presents a change to that state, our minds will go into defense mode, working to ensure that our internal sameness is maintained. It will lie, cheat, and convince us of whatever it has to in order to ensure our safety. This is great when we are in actual danger. But the brain doesn't base decisions on truth with a capital "T," but rather our perception of reality at the moment. This perception is heavily influenced by our internal monsters.

How does our brain lie to us? It uses what I like to refer to as "cons," specific thoughts that lead our conscious mind to misperceptions and cognitive errors. There are seven cons that our brain regularly utilizes to convince us of the "truth" of a particular cognition error. Together, these cons work to achieve one thing—to keep us safe by maintaining the status quo, even when we are not in danger and have a high motivation to change.

Here's a look at the specific cons our brain uses to maintain our stress and anxiety and resist changes to our specific adaptation, no matter how ineffective.

➤➤ *"The Sky is Falling" Con*

Have you heard of Chicken Little? Every time an acorn fell on his head from the big oak tree above him, he mistakenly thought the sky was falling. No matter what anyone told him, no matter all of the evidence to the contrary, Chicken Little honestly believed the sky was falling. This powerful con works in much the same way. And just like Chicken Little, when your brain engages this con, you will believe its message that the worst is going to happen. No matter what!

Also referred to as catastrophic thinking, when this con is engaged, your brain convinces you that the absolute worst is about to happen. If your heart is beating fast, your brain says you are having a heart attack. If you see a small leak in your roof, your brain says the entire roof is about to collapse. This con is rooted in your fear and uses your fear narrative to get you to avoid whatever is the trigger. Anxiety is all about avoidance and fear, and this con optimizes both.

➤➤ *"The Black and White" Con*

This is a con about absolutes—things are absolutely fabulous or absolutely horrible. There is nothing in between. Life, however, is seldom so finite. We don't typically operate in black-and-white terms, but exist in many shades of gray. The Black and White Con, also known as all-or-nothing thinking, relies on your acceptance and preference for absolutes. With this con, you immediately go to extremes. Either you feel fantastic, or you are on the verge of a panic attack. You are either successful, or you fail miserably. This con does not focus on the process or journey of life at all. Instead, it concerns itself with only the absolutes. It is rigid and unyielding, demanding your attention because of its insistence that you also view the world in this way.

➤➤ *"The Pessimist's Code" Con*

Did you know that pessimism and optimism are a choice? They are. Recent research in the field of positive psychology has determined that people can choose optimism and, in doing so, negate the negative impact of stress and anxiety. That is, unless your brain is running The Pessimist's Code on you. With this con, your mind holds a negative mindset toward everything. No matter what positive thing may be happening, this con is waiting for the other shoe to drop, choosing to highlight only the negatives within each positive.

People who live with increased stress and anxiety often develop a hyper-sensitive threat perception. They see danger around every corner and with every change to their internal physical state. That's where this con comes into play. Rather than allow you to rationalize through these changes and focus on neutral or positive events, The Pessimist's Code overemphasizes potential adverse outcomes and threats at the expense of anything else.

⇥ "The Perfectionist's Mantra" Con

Similar to The Black and White Con, The Perfectionist's Mantra focuses on all-or-nothing thinking by overemphasizing flaws and failures in comparison to strengths and achievements. By minimizing any successes, this con keeps you trapped in believing that you can't change, even if you think you "should." The constant overexaggeration of your "flaws" provides a powerful and paralyzing effect on your strengths, undermining your confidence and resilience over time.

⇥ "The Negative Label" Con

One of the most powerful cons in your brain's arsenal is The Negative Label Con. This con allows the brain to attach a negative label to yourself, or an aspect of yourself. Like the cons before, attaching a negative label serves to undermine confidence and maintain status quo. It's important to remember that the cons are subtle. It may seem reasonable during an anxiety attack to want to call yourself "stupid" or "weak." But it's important to recognize that these are cognition errors and ultimately do not serve you well.

⇥ "The Fortune Teller" Con

Everyone loves the fortune-telling machine at the local fair, predicting our future with no basis in reality. It's fun. Until your brain uses the same technique as a con to get you to remain locked in your anxiety and stress. The Fortune Teller Con combines The Sky Is Falling Con with The Black and White Con, telling you that everything will always turn out for the worst. Messages like "I'll never pass the class" and "We'll never get to the concert in time" permeate every thought, despite having no actual reason to believe the accuracy of the con. By engaging this con, your brain is able to wear you down and maintain the status quo again. There is no need to try if you always know the outcome is going to be bad. The con promotes and enhances a fixed mindset.

⋙ "The Victim's Rant" Con

The final con in your brain's rather extensive arsenal is The Victim's Rant. Also known as blaming, this con is based on the idea that you are a victim of your situation. Someone else is always to blame for the things that happen in your life. If you get a bad grade, it is because the teacher failed to explain what would be on the test. If you weren't named captain, it is because your coach hates you. If you got into a fight with your boyfriend, it's because he refused to listen to you or see your perspective.

Although this reasoning may be partially correct, being a victim in your life abdicates any ability to break free from your anxiety. You relinquish your control over your life and give yourself permission to unintentionally create your reality by succumbing to your faulty thinking. This is not to say that there aren't hardships that limit choices and the autonomy you may feel over your life—there are. But, within each circumstance, there is one thing that is seldom limited, and that is your thinking.

The seven cons represent the main ways your brain can trick you into making cognition errors that keep you locked in your anxious thinking and patterns of behavior. In the next chapter, we will examine ways to counteract the cons and break free from thinking patterns that do not serve you. But first, it is important to recognize how these cons show up in your life.

Take a moment to complete Activity 17: The Seven Cons with examples from your own life. Consider a time when you felt anxiety. What were you thinking? What cons did your brain offer as a way to keep you locked in your homeostatic state?

If you're struggling to think of the ways your brain has delivered these cons to you, use your inner persona you created and imagine what your mind might say to her. It's okay if it isn't entirely accurate at this point. Just try to complete the exercise as best you can (and yes, it is likely that one of the cons will show up as you work on the task!).

Once you recognize the ways the seven cons show up in your life, it is time to try to identify the cons in action. Think back to a time when you experienced high levels of stress or anxiety this week. What self-talk were

THE SEVEN CONS

Directions: For each con, write in one example from your own thoughts. You can make it up if you can't think of one that you've thought of before.

Con	Description	Personal Example
The Sky Is Falling	You make the situation bigger than it is and imagine the absolute worst thing is about to happen.	*Jason hasn't responded to my text. He must be seeing someone else behind my back.*
The Black and White	You view everything as always great or always horrible.	
The Pessimist's Code	Your threat perception is hyperaware, so you only see the negative in any situation.	
The Perfectionist's Mantra	You focus on what you consider your flaws and minimize any acknowledgement of your strengths.	
The Negative Label	You label yourself in harshly negative ways, focusing on small aspects of self.	
The Fortune Teller	You tell yourself what other people are thinking about you—and always in the most negative of ways.	
The Victim's Rant	You blame other people for everything that happens, keeping yourself as the forever-victim.	

you engaged in? What cons was your brain using to maintain the status quo? Why did it think you needed to be safe?

Complete Activity 18: Recognizing the Cons whenever you experience anxiety or feel your internal monsters at work. This is the first step to understanding how to unravel the con and recognize your cognition errors. Using the skill of witnessing along with this exercise will help you to recognize the cognition errors you are making. For many people, these errors become habitual. The more you can recognize your typical thinking patterns, the quicker you can replace your thoughts, feelings, and behaviors with more adaptive approaches to life's stressful situations.

Exploring the Minefield

It often feels like anxiety and panic attacks happen without warning. This is seldom ever the case. More often than not, there are subtle indicators that an attack is imminent. We simply must train ourselves to be observers of behavior, to witness our thoughts, feelings, and actions.

Think about a time when you experienced an anxious response. You can also use one of the events you described in Activity 8 or 9 in Chapter 3. What happened just before you experienced the event? Did someone ask something of you? Did you respond to something you heard or saw or smelled? Were you thinking of something specific? Often times, our environment and our inner dialogues trigger anxious behavior.

The more often we experience anxiety, and the more we struggle with anxious responses, the more sensitive our brain becomes to perceptions of threat. All things begin to signal danger. A distinct tone of voice from a friend, the actions or nonactions of a family member, even a once enjoyable activity can become interpreted as a dangerous event. When this happens, it triggers a particular pattern of response. Our habituated stress response takes over, and we react strongly. This reaction starts the cycle of anxiety and avoidance, leading to a more sensitive threat perception.

To break the cycle and change your response, you need to begin to understand what triggers you. Take a minute and complete Activity 19: My Triggers. Using your witnessing skills, begin to identify those things that frequently trigger an anxious response. Try to include triggers from your environment, as well as thoughts from your internal monsters and fear narrative.

ACTIVITY 18 ⇐

RECOGNIZING THE CONS

Directions: Reflect on a time of heightened anxiety. What happened? What were you thinking? What con was your brain initiating? Remember, often more than one con can be seen at any given time.

Event	My Self-Talk	Name The Con(s)	Why Do I Need It?
Example: I get a test back and scored a B. Immediately, my throat feels like it's closing and my stomach tosses. I am certain I will be sick, so I excuse myself from class to go to the restroom.	I am so stupid. I should've studied more. A B is horrible. I'll never pass my class now!	The Negative Label and The Perfectionist's Mantra. The Black and White Con is at the end as well.	I struggle feeling safe when I experience even the most minor failure. I think I won't amount to anything if I don't get straight A's.

Take a moment to reflect on your answers above. What do you notice about your thinking?

_____

_____

_____

_____

MY TRIGGERS

Directions: Think about your anxiety. Using your witnessing skills, determine the things that trigger an anxious response. Consider both internal and external triggers. After you've determined what triggers you, complete the rest of the worksheet. You may not have all of the answers yet, but as you continue through the book, this type of task will get easier.

Triggering Event/ Activity	How I Respond	Cons?
Example: Internal trigger: Feeling worried.	I begin to imagine the worst thing happening.	Sky Is Falling

Note. Adapted from *Raising the Shy Child: A Parent's Guide to Social Anxiety* (p. 107), by C. Fonseca, 2015, Waco, TX: Prufrock Press. Copyright 2015 by Prufrock Press. Adapted with permission.

Once you've completed the worksheet, think about how your mental cons and triggers work together. Are there specific cons your mind uses in response to specific triggers? How would rephrasing your cons change your triggers? In the next chapter, you'll have an opportunity to reframe both your triggers and your cons. By doing both, you will have an opportunity to change how you interpret your mind and experience your anxiety.

Seung's Story

I don't remember a time when I didn't feel anxious. Being a first generation American, I felt a lot of pressure to succeed. My parents moved here from South Korea, seeking opportunities that weren't available there. They raised me to believe that hard work was expected and success was nonnegotiable, especially when it came to school.

Middle school was not much of a challenge. I breezed through my classes, earning top grades. Although the curriculum wasn't demanding, I insisted on working hard and making certain every assignment represented my best effort. In addition to the coursework, I was involved in tennis and music. It was stressful keeping up with everything, but it was what was expected.

High school was more challenging. I participated in the International Baccalaureate program. The workload was harder than middle school, the pressure to succeed was overwhelming. Each week that passed brought with it more pressure, more competition. Eventually, it was too much.

In the early winter of my first semester, I could barely handle everything. My mind constantly raced, filling me with negative thoughts.

"You will never succeed if you don't get A's."

"Look at all of those comments. You are so dumb."

"If I fail this test, I will disappoint my family."

Each phrase tossed around my mind. It all felt like truth. I believed each and every statement. The more the phrases continued, the more I was certain I would fail. I studied harder, stayed up longer, worked more. But none of it helped. The phrases grew louder until I felt paralyzed.

My grades were not improving, despite my efforts. The competition within the classes was increasing. I was beginning to fall apart.

Everything boiled over by the end of the year. Stressed out beyond words and convinced that I had to achieve top marks on every test or I would fail out of school (the truth was I was earning an A/B average and in no danger of failing out), I pushed harder and harder.

Until I broke.

It happened quickly. The mean phrases circled my brain constantly until I could no longer function at all. I thought about quitting, maybe even disappearing all together. My parents asked if I was okay every morning. And every morning I lied and said I was fine.

My friends grew concerned. Although being overly stressed was common in the IB program, I was taking it to an extreme. My teachers started to suspect something was wrong. One teacher approached me and expressed his concern. He offered me a choice—speak to the counselor or my family, or he would. I needed help.

The school psychologist was great. She talked to me about emotional upheaval and overwhelming feelings. She introduced the idea that my brain was giving me messages that weren't accurate. These negative thoughts were not "truth" necessarily, but rather inaccurate messages designed to keep me in a state of stress. I didn't really understand at that time why that could happen (something I now see), but it didn't matter. Everything the psychologist was saying resonated with me.

I told my parents about the stress and my feelings. Instead of disappointing them, they said they understood and just wanted me to "get better."

I started seeing a counselor. Over the summer, I slowly learned how to differentiate my thoughts, which ones I should listen to versus which ones were not accurate. By the time the next school year started, I was feeling better. I had learned the beginnings of what would become a habit for me—discerning thoughts and managing intense emotions.

I can't say the road has been easy. There are still times when I get overwhelmed, when my brain runs amuck and engages in a lot of negative self-talk. But I have learned that this isn't "truth." I have a few strategies to help me now. I have learned that I have naturally intense emotions, which can trigger high levels of anxiety from time to time. My negative self-talk goes into overdrive when this occurs. But it doesn't derail me anymore. I have strategies that help

Our brain works hard to maintain balance and integrate information in the most concise and efficient way, all with a goal of survival. It'll do almost anything to maintain homeostasis, even if that state does not serve us well. And, it has many tricks in its arsenal to accomplish this goal, including cons and misdirection. Many times these mixed messages result in fear behavior and anxious responses. Our job is to learn to discover when this behavior is appropriate for the situation and when it serves only the inaccurate messages of our inner selves. By becoming aware of our internal dialogue, we can begin to understand the purpose of our anxious monsters. Only then can we dismantle faulty thinking and replace our cognition errors with messages that serve us better and increase our personal resilience.

Over the next few chapters, we'll examine the ways we can tame the internal monsters and reframe our thinking. For now, take a few moments to explore the reflection questions below and discover how your mind gives you inaccurate messages.

Do the Work

Use the questions below to bring you to a deeper understanding of your thoughts and feelings about the information in this chapter.

- What role do the mental cons currently play in my life? Are there one or two cons that show up most frequently?
- What are my core safety issues; what things do I feel I need the most protection from? How do my cons protect me and keep me safe?
- What message do I want to give to myself about my anxiety? What other ways should my brain try to keep me safe?
- What strategies can I use to recognize and discern when I need to listen to my internal thoughts and when I need to consider changing the message?
- What can I do right now to rewrite internal messages and thought patterns that no longer serve me?

Chapter 5

CONTROLLING THE SPIN

    I mentioned in the last chapter that the first step toward releasing the hold anxiety had on my life was recognizing the ways my brain worked to keep me anxious. Once my awareness increased, I had to learn how to respond to my anxiety. Initially, I struggled, attempting to wage war with the inner beasts. Every time I felt attacked, I responded in kind, usually increasing my anxious feelings. When my actions didn't work as I'd hoped, I tried ignoring everything—my feelings, the incessant thoughts, all of it. The result was no better.

    I had to find a new way to face my anxiety. Attacking it didn't work. Going around wasn't a solution. I needed to learn how to go *through* the anxiety, how to embrace what was happening from a place of nonjudgmental discernment and create a new narrative about my stress and anxiety.

    In this chapter, you will learn what it means to lean into the feelings and change your personal story of stress and anxiety. The exercises are designed to build awareness, change your inner tolerance for stress-producing situations, and adjust your thoughts. You'll begin to recognize the ways your brain works to protect you from perceived threats, and how to rewrite personal definitions of "threat." Finally, you'll begin to chronicle your subtle victories, creating a new internal script.

Live Within the Feeling

In the last chapter, I referred to anxiety as a disease of avoidance. Our difficulty living in moments of anxiety coupled with habituated fear responses often worsen our anxious behaviors over time. Developing a tolerance for the feeling of anxiety, as well as neutralizing the triggers, can often provide the space we need to retrain our thinking.

Psychologists often refer to tolerance training as *exposure*. Classic exposure is based on the idea that the more we are exposed to the thing we fear, the less we are afraid of it. Think back to your own life. As a child, you were most likely afraid of the dark and monsters under the bed. But as you grew older, as your tolerance for darkness increased, and as much of your fear disappeared, your rational brain learned that the things in the dark were the same as the things in the light—it was just a matter of perspective. You would not have been able to learn this, however, had you not developed a tolerance for being in the dark.

Exposure is typically achieved in one of three ways: (1) experiencing a hierarchy of your fear, starting with the least impactful and moving to the greatest; (2) exposing yourself to your greatest fear all at once; and (3) suppressing fear responses. All three strategies work by changing your tolerance for anxiety and the thing you fear. Typically, psychologists and self-help books recommend #1 or #3, or a combination of both. The second strategy, also known as flooding, can be highly traumatic. I would recommend only engaging in that strategy with a trained professional.

Let me take a moment to explain each approach and provide examples and practice. The first strategy, desensitization, involves creating a hierarchy of your fear. For example, if you are afraid of speaking in front of the class, your hierarchy may begin with talking to a friend or into a recording device. After you've mastered that step, you'd try speaking to the teacher, eventually leading to speaking in front of the class. Each step along the hierarchy would move closer toward giving your speech. Once you've developed a hierarchy, you begin to expose yourself to each step on the list, taking time to calm your mind, your feelings, and your body with each progressive step. In the example given above, you would practice a calming strategy before, during, and after speaking with a friend. You would follow this routine for each of the steps on the hierarchy. Each step would require you to maintain inner calm before moving on. In this way, you are creating a new internal experience of the event. As we've previously discovered, your brain grows and learns after each experience with stress. Exposure not only builds tolerance for something through the normalization of that activity, but it creates an entirely new experience as well.

It is important that you have learned a variety of relaxation techniques before trying this strategy. Chapter 8 provides several strategies you can combine with this exercise. Desensitization will not work if you remain stressed at each level. It is vital that you achieve a calm before moving to a more intense activity on your hierarchy.

It's important to note that exposure can work with cognitive events as well as things occurring in real time. Visualizing each event can have a similar impact to direct experience. This is particularly true with the second strategy, flooding. Flooding is when we expose ourselves to our deepest fears all at once. As I mentioned earlier, flooding is best done in partnership with a mental health professional. But the visualization strategies can be helpful with the desensitization.

Try this exercise. Imagine something that creates moderate levels of anxiety. Picture it in detail in your mind. What do you notice with your body? Are you slipping into a fight-or-flight response? If you are, take a moment to relax. Notice your breath, feel your body release tension, and quiet your mind. Try the exercise again. Continue to visualize the event until you no longer react with anxiety. Activity 20: Normalizing My Fear provides step-by-step instructions to create your hierarchy and move through desensitization.

I mentioned earlier that many of our stress responses become habituated over time. This creates a compulsion, of sort, to act a certain way when faced with anxious situations. It's hard to change the avoidance-anxiety cycle when we are engaging in habitual responses. It's important, therefore, to break the routine of our behaviors.

Consider this scenario. You experience a high level of stress. Your throat begins to close and you panic. You call your best friend and suddenly you can breathe. Your fear subsides. A few days later you feel stress again. Once again, your throat begins to close and you panic. Because calling your friend worked last time, you try it again. It works. A cycle begins. Your brain has decided that the only way to get relief, to change the feeling, is to call

ACTIVITY 20 ⇜

NORMALIZING MY FEAR

Directions: Use this guide to learn how to utilize exposure strategies. Follow each step outlined below. Please note that this should only be done with low-level anxiety unless this is being done in cooperation with a counselor or therapist. When done correctly, this is a powerful way to retrain your reaction to stressful stimuli.

1. Write down your biggest fear. *Example: Speaking in front of the class.*
2. Make a list of related activities, starting with the least anxiety-provoking and ending with the fear listed above. *Speaking into a recorder, speaking to a classmate, speaking to the teacher, speaking in front of a small group, speaking in front of the class.*
3. Starting with the activity that causes the least anxiety, begin to complete each task. *Speaking into a recorder.*
4. Pay attention to your anxiety as you complete the task. If you begin to experience anxiety, stop and use a calming activity until you are calm. Try the task again. Do not move to the next task until you are able to do the activity with minimal stress or anxiety.
5. Continue moving through each activity until you are able to successfully face your initial fear.
6. Celebrate each success, no matter how small, as you progress through this activity. Use the "Jumps Toward Joy" activity (p. 88) to help.

Note. Adapted from *Raising the Shy Child: A Parent's Guide to Social Anxiety* (p. 173), by C. Fonseca, 2015, Waco, TX: Prufrock Press. Copyright 2015 by Prufrock Press. Adapted with permission.

your friend. Over and over, you call your friend to get relief from your feelings of panic. Your response is habituated.

But the story doesn't end there. As you begin to release yourself from the bonds of anxiety, you discover that calling your friend is based on a false truth. There is no real connection between your friend and your stress. Furthermore, you discover that the sensation of your throat closing isn't a threat at all. It is simply an indication that your stress levels are increasing. Taking a moment to relax is all that's needed to calm down and change your stress response.

You decide to practice being calm in response to your stress instead of calling your friend. Not only is this a more helpful, or adaptive, reaction based on your internal strength, but it releases the stress your constant calls have put on the friendship itself. So, the next time you feel anxious you test out your theory. You calm your mind and it works; you don't need your friend to relieve the stress.

However, due to the habituated response of calling your friend you are compelled to call, even though you know the action of calling your friend may create a false message of alarm again. The compulsion to call is strong. That's because one of the cons is in charge. The old brain is fighting hard, using your habituated responses to maintain the status quo and not integrate the new change.

Suppressing your fear response is a way to fight off the urge to engage in behavior that doesn't serve you. By tolerating the increased anxiety that occurs when you ignore your compulsion, you teach the brain that you didn't need to call in the first place. You strengthen the positive changes and build a new internal narrative.

Take a look at Activity 21: Changing My Response. Take a moment to think about the habitual responses that you continue even when they are no longer needed. Which ones can you change? Why? As you work through the activity, think of ways you can develop a healthier response to anxious feelings.

It is important to note that suppressing responses is not effective with a full-blown panic attack. In fact, the anxiety produced when suppressing responses can increase the intensity of panic by triggering your fear narrative. You will need to learn discernment to know when to utilize a response suppression technique. If you are working with a mental health professional, he or she can assist with this.

In the next section, we'll continue to explore ways you can change the internal messages of your anxiety and fear and break your habitual responses.

Override Your Thoughts

Psychologists refer to our errors in thinking using a variety of terms: cognition errors, automatic negative thoughts, and the cons I discussed at length in Chapter 4. Each of these terms refers to the mistaken beliefs we often hold—beliefs that are usually rooted in our fears and continued due to the intense emotions we are feeling.

There are a number of ways to combat cognition errors. Recognizing the cons and reframing them into adaptive or empowering thoughts, as described in Chapters 3 and 4, is one way. Another is something I like to call *proof*. Developed first for use in *Emotional Intensity in Gifted Students*

ACTIVITY 21 ✑

CHANGING MY RESPONSE

Directions: Think about your most recent reactions to anxiety. Complete the worksheet below each time you engage in a stress/anxiety response.

Event	My Response	Why I Responded That Way	What I Want to Do Instead	How Will I Do It?
Example: Mom asked me to clean my room.	I yelled at her and stomped out of the room.	I was stressed/anxious due to a test.	Tell Mom about the test and ask her if I can clean my room tomorrow.	• Take a deep breath. • Count to 5 before I speak. • Ask Mom if I can talk to her. • Have a conversation about the test. Ask if I can put off cleaning my room. • Accept whatever answer I receive.

(Fonseca, 2016), I use proof as a way to help people learn to discern their thinking and recognize cognition errors as they are occurring.

The technique is simple and similar to Activity 18: Recognizing the Cons. Every time you have a significant negative thought related to your anxiety, I want you to challenge it and ask yourself to "prove it." For example, if you believe you are horrible at math and therefore will never pass the class, look for solid proof that this is the truth. Are you failing every test? Have you ever passed a math class at all? Have you ever understood a concept in math, even when you were younger? By going through this process, you are helping to shine the light inward and expose faulty thinking patterns.

In Activity 22: Prove It!, I've combined proof with the cons. Take a few minutes to review the cons you've identified with Activity 18: Recognizing the Cons. Go through each one and look for proof that the con is accurate. Write a reframing or empowering statement for each inaccurate thought.

Another strategy for correcting faulty thinking and your cons is to use the empowering questions discussed in Chapter 2. Every time you look inward and watch what your inner persona is doing, what she is saying and believing, you have an opportunity to correct cognition errors. Think of yourself as the director of a play. Your inner persona is one of the actors. Your job is to recognize when she has the script wrong and correct it. It is the same in your mind. In Activity 23: Director's Notes, you will practice correcting the cognition errors you are experiencing. The more experience you have rewriting your internal scripts, the more you will be able to change your responses to anxious feelings.

Table 3, Strategies to Correct Cognition Errors, lists the variety of exercises throughout the book that will help you practice this skill.

The final exercise I want to give you in this section focuses on something Dr. David Burns referred to as hidden emotions in his book *When Panic Attacks*. He referred to anxiety as a "niceness disease," born, at least partially, out of our reluctance as women to be assertive (Burns, 2006, p. 25).

A result of our social conditioning, many girls and women lack strong assertiveness skills. We hide our true emotions behind a mask of niceness and people-pleasing behaviors. Instead of owning our feelings, we play the ultimate game of avoidance and just discount our feelings altogether. And we are often rewarded for it. Niceness is seen as a positive attribute, while assertiveness or emotional intensity is consistently viewed more negatively, especially in women.

ACTIVITY 22 ⇐
PROVE IT!

Directions: Review your cons from Activity 18: Recognizing the Cons. Write down each con, along with any proof that the con is correct or incorrect. For each con, write an empowering statement.

Thought and Con	Truth	Empowering Statement
Example: I'm horrible at calculus. I will never ever be able to learn this stuff. (Black and White Con)	This is the first time I am taking this class. My grades are slowly improving with each test.	Although calculus is hard, I am understanding more each day. With practice and effort, I will continue to get better at it.

DIRECTOR'S NOTES

Directions: Imagine that you are the director of a play and your inner persona is one of your actors. She consistently demonstrates mistakes in motivation or internal thoughts. You help by giving her director's notes, or empowering questions, to help her reframe her thinking. Complete the chart below with the action, your persona's thoughts, and your director's notes (empowering questions and answers).

Event/Action	Persona's Thoughts	Empowering Questions/Statements
Example: Swim meet	"I am never going to swim fast enough. This is too hard."	♦ What is one thing you can do to do well in the meet?—You can practice more. You can practice relaxation strategies. ♦ Have you been successful at meets before?—Yes, I generally do well, even though I am nervous.

TABLE 3
Strategies to Correct Cognition Errors

Below is a list of strategies to correct faulty thinking that often occurs when your cons are in charge. You will have a chance to practice each strategy as you go through the book.

Skill	Activity	
Identify errors in thinking	♦ How I React to Stress ♦ Witnessing ♦ A Day In the Life ♦ The Seven Cons ♦ Recognizing the Cons ♦ My Triggers	♦ Prove It! ♦ Director's Notes ♦ My True Feelings ♦ My Thoughts About Panic ♦ My Fear Narrative
Replace cognition errors	♦ Changing My Response ♦ Prove It! ♦ Recognizing the Cons	♦ Director's Notes ♦ Shifting Thoughts ♦ My Inner Experts
Mindsets	♦ The Positive Side of Stress ♦ How Stress Serves Me ♦ Normalize My Fear ♦ Prove It! ♦ Jumps Toward Joy	♦ Thank You ♦ What Do I Desire ♦ Insane Courage ♦ Dear Me ♦ I Love Me
Empowering statements	♦ I Choose ♦ I've Got This ♦ Prove It!	♦ Director's Notes ♦ My Empowering Statements ♦ My Inner Experts

Developing assertiveness skills involves clear communication, self-confidence, self- and social-awareness, and self-management—the same skills needed to manage anxiety. Using the strategies for correcting cognition errors is a great way to start.

Begin by observing your inner persona. What is she "really" feeling? What does she want? I find it is easiest to do this in my journal, but Activity 24: My True Feelings works well too. Pose the question, wait for a moment, and write the first response that comes to your head without thinking. Many times you'll uncover a simple annoyance that is at the heart of the issue. Sometimes there is a deeper issue to examine. Do this as often as needed until you uncover your hidden emotions.

Once you've figured out what you are feeling and what you want, it is time to solve the problem. This is where you may need to muster up some

MY TRUE FEELINGS

Directions: Complete the chart whenever you have a response that is bigger than it should be.

Behavior—"What Did I Do?"	Initial Thought/Feeling	"Is This Really What I'm Feeling?" Yes / No	New Thought/Feeling	"Is This Really What I'm Feeling?" Yes / No
Example: I was asked to redo a project.	Frustration and anger	Not fully	Disappointment ("I should have done better") and anger ("I wish you'd told me what you wanted the first time")	Yes

courage. You will likely have to ask someone for what you want or assert yourself in some way. And your stress or anxiety will likely rise for a moment.

Remember the stress responses from Chapters 1 and 2. Tell yourself that the anxiety is just stress, urging you to act. Review Activity 5: The Positive Side of Stress from Chapter 2. Look at the ways your stress response can serve you now. Choose to use your "challenge" response to encourage your self-advocacy skills. Use the tend-and-befriend response to muster up your courage. As you begin to get a clear picture of your true feelings and start to meet your needs, anxiety will lessen and you will naturally strengthen your positive messages toward stress.

Release and Renew

Learning to manage and move past anxiety is an intense process. You will have good days and not-so-good days. It's important to remember to celebrate little successes. Every time you resist listening to your cons; each time you release negative thought patterns; whenever you reframe negative, limiting beliefs into positive, growth-oriented mindsets, you are taking large steps on the road to releasing the hold of anxiety forever. Likewise, every time you believe the con and each time you are limited by your thoughts, you strengthen anxiety's grip on your life.

As you work toward making more positive steps, it is very easy to fall back into the trap of anxiety. Sometimes this is due to your brain's desire to maintain the status quo. Remember how I said your brain would do anything to resist change? Maintaining the status quo isn't the only reason why you may take a step backward. Sometimes a slip is due to a new skill that is not yet solidified. Sometimes we are just experiencing a habit.

Poet Portia Nelson (2002) described the process of recovery beautifully in her poem "An Autobiography in Five Short Chapters." Through the poem, the main character experiences anxious behavior, first as a result of an accident and then by habit until she eventually changes her behavior. This poem has been considered a seminal example of the road toward recovery.

The point of Nelson's words is simple: Recovery is a process. If you continue to show up and do the work, you will change your thoughts, feelings, and behaviors. Anxiety won't always direct you.

One of the best ways to stay motivated as you begin to let go of anxiety is through the celebration of successes. Track the little wins, the minor victories. Express gratitude for the entire process. Embrace the aspects of the stress cycle that build courage and joy.

To help, I've created an activity (Activity 25) my good friend Joelle calls "Jumps Toward Joy." Write down what you did, how that action moved you in a helpful direction, and how you felt about it. As you begin to recognize these moments and embrace the new you, you give your brain permission to shed the old stories. Each step on the road to release adds to your forward momentum. Each time you pay more attention to your accomplishments, you create the space needed to accomplish more. Moment by moment, you are creating a new narrative.

Before leaving this section, I think it's important to take a moment to evaluate where you are in your stress and anxiety thinking. Review the quizzes that start Parts I and II. Have your answers changed? Are you beginning to shift your thinking?

As change occurs, it is easy to get frustrated with minor setbacks. When this happens and we engage in our old patterns of behavior, we may find ourselves experiencing increases in stress and anxiety. It's important to stop and recognize what is happening. The activities in Part III can help. Mindfulness, relaxation, and optimism will help you recover from minor setbacks, as well as the overwhelming feelings that result from major, stress-filled events. Additionally, engaging in a gratitude activity can quickly remind you of the progress you've made.

For Activity 26: Thank You, I'd like you to write a note to the inner persona you created earlier. Thank her for everything she has done for you, the way she's handled stress, and how she's kept you safe. By acknowledging what she has done and the role she has played in your life, you are creating the opportunity to move forward and experience more joy.

Try this activity whenever you find it difficult to recognize another con or let go of another faulty thought. By offering gratitude to where you've been, you make the journey forward possible.

ACTIVITY 25

JUMPS TOWARD JOY

Directions: Take a moment to think about the ways you have grown throughout the process of working through this book. Fill in each of your "wins," no matter how small. Celebrate each time you are successful, each little jump toward joy on the Road to Release!

What I Did	How It Improved/Changed My Thinking	How I Feel About It
Example: I recognized how I was using The Pessimist's Code Con in my math class.	By recognizing it, I was able to shift my thinking.	Really good. Empowered because I could change my thinking.

THANK YOU

Directions: Take a moment to thank your inner self, the inner persona you have been getting to know—she has been working hard to keep you safe.

Dear (inner persona):
Thank you so much for _____

_____

_____

_____

_____

_____

_____

_____

_____

_____

_____

_____

_____

_____

_____

_____

_____

_____

_____

_____

_____

_____

_____

Stress and anxiety, I've lived with both forever. In elementary school, I got sick before every test. In middle school, I went to the nurse's office whenever I had to speak in class. And now, in high school, I often wonder if I am just destined to feel anxious thoughts forever.

I've tried a lot of ways to relieve the anxiety—ignoring my thoughts, pushing through the feelings, a variety of coping strategies like deep breathing—but nothing worked for long.

I am trying something different this year. I am paying attention to the "whole" me. It started with a conversation with my school counselor at the end of the last school year. She is a bit of a health nut and always talking about eating healthy, sleeping well, and mindfulness.

I had been visiting her office weekly throughout the year because of my anxiety. She always gave good advice about ways to think about my stress and release my negative thoughts. Her advice worked in the short term, but never for more than a week or so.

On a particularly hard day after finals, my counselor asked me to try a few things over the summer break—mindfulness, 30 minutes of daily exercise, and eating healthy. I'll be honest, my first thought was "Whatever! What difference is this going to make?" I didn't believe a little deep breathing, walking, or paying attention to the caffeine and sugar I ate would make any difference. I was wrong.

I diligently did everything the counselor suggested. I sat for 5 minutes and focused on my breathing. I swam and walked 30 minutes each day. And I ate well-balanced meals. Giving up caffeine was tough, but I did switch my iced coffees for iced green tea.

The first thing I noticed was increased awareness of my stress and anxiety. I also noticed that I was able to relax more quickly than I had ever been able to relax before the summer. I continued the healthy strategies well into my junior year. Things are still hard at times. The difference is that I feel more able to handle my stress.

I don't know if the suggestions from my counselor are the reason things are easier. I just know I feel better than I've felt in a very, very long time. Don't get me wrong. An iced drink on a hot day is fantastic. I just add mindfulness and a brisk swim. For me, it's about balance—the more balanced I feel, the more I can handle the stress I experience.

Throughout this chapter, you explored a large variety of ways to address your thinking around anxiety. Reframing your internal messages is hard work, but it is the necessary action you must take if you truly want to break free from your cycle of anxious responses.

Sometimes we are unable to manage our anxiety before it slips away from us, transforming into significant emotional upheaval and panic. The next chapter discusses the reality of panic and intense emotional responses. Before you jump into that information, take a moment to reflect on the exercises throughout this chapter. Use the reflection questions to develop a pattern of reframing and reprogramming your reactions to stress and anxiety. You will not always be able to prevent highly stressful situations from occurring, nor will you always be able to avoid an anxious response. But you can learn to manage your emotions and reframe your thinking before habituating the anxiety.

Do the Work

Use the questions below to bring you to a deeper understanding of your thoughts and feelings about the information in this chapter. Consider focusing on one or two topics every time you journal.

- What is my typical response to periods of significant anxiety? What would happen if I no longer reacted that way? Imagine what it would feel like to no longer react negatively to the feeling of anxiety.
- When I see the phrase "live within the feeling," what feelings come to mind? Are there any stress points in my body when I read the words aloud? Describe them.
- Have I been able to release my anxiety in the past? How did I accomplish it? What would happen if I released it again?
- Write a letter to my anxiety. What do I want to tell it?
- What can I do right now to embrace a different experience with my anxiety?

Chapter 6

RIDING THE WAVE OF PANIC

My first experience with a panic attack happened when I was 11. My parents and I were learning to scuba dive and had our first ocean dive. The week before, we went to the dive shop and picked out our supplies: wet suits, mask and fins, weights, and the tanks. We were excited. A little scared, but mostly excited. The day of the dive, we left the house before dawn. Sunrise hit as we boarded the boat that would take us to the nearby island of Catalina. By the time we got there, the morning haze had given way to a beautiful California morning.

My dad was the first to enter the water. I followed. The tanks and weights felt heavy. My heart pounded as I took a large step off of the side of the boat. I submerged briefly before bobbing to the surface, excited and alive. I'd waited for this day forever. I was going on my first dive. I would get to see the world I only knew about from the books that crowded my desk at home.

My mom was the last of us to enter the water. Like me, she took a giant leap off the side of the boat. She sank briefly before bobbing back to the surface. But she didn't look excited, as I had. She looked terrified.

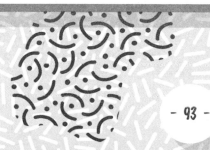

Unable to breathe, her eyes wide and expression gaunt, my mother looked like she was about to faint. My dad reached her first, followed by the dive masters. I stayed back and watched, horrified.

"Can't . . . breathe . . ." my mother would repeat over and over. Her speech was clipped; her voice, breathless. Whatever was happening was bad.

The dive masters got Mom back to the boat quickly. Dad and I continued the dive. But the image of my mom in the throes of a panic attack have never left me. In that moment, she believed something bad, something threatening, was happening. In retrospect, she understood that she was gravely afraid and the threat was imagined.

This is the world of panic.

Fear is a primal emotion, designed to signal potential life-threatening harm and motivate us into action that leads to our survival. In truth, it is much more. Fear is responsible for many of our most maladaptive behaviors. And fear prevents many of our health-producing responses. In short, fear can be part of our problem.

American alternative rock band Papa Roach is credited with the phrase "face everything and rise," a strong meaning to the acronym F.E.A.R. (Shaddix, Esperance, & Churko, 2014). The songwriters believe in the importance of facing your problems and rewriting your story of fear and pain. It is a great alternative to the meaning of the word *fear*, one we will explore throughout this chapter.

After exploring the specifics of what panic is and how fear relates to it, you will explore the role fear has in your life—your fear narrative. You will also have the opportunity to practice rewriting your narrative, as well as exploring other common strategies to help you move past episodes of panic and severe anxiety.

When Anxiety Turns Into Panic

Sudden and extreme anxiety attacks are typically referred to as panic attacks. As the name would suggest, it feels like an attack on your entire stress system. You don't feel heart palpitations or shortness of breath. You don't feel dizzy or numb. You're not afraid or anxious. You are all of these things at once.

Psychologists define a panic attack as the presence of four or more anxiety symptoms occurring at the same time (see Table 4 for the symptoms). A panic disorder is diagnosed when you have several panic attacks over a short

TABLE 4
Panic Attack Symptom List

Below are the typical symptoms of panic. They overlap with the symptoms of stress and anxiety. What distinguishes them as panic is both their sudden onset and the intensity with which these symptoms strike.

◆ Shortness of breath	◆ Nausea	◆ Intense fear of dying
◆ Heart palpitations	◆ Choking sensation	◆ Intense fear of "going crazy"
◆ Dizziness	◆ Mental detachment	
◆ Faintness	◆ Trembling/shaking	

period of time and you have experienced what psychologists referred to as "anticipatory anxiety" (Bourne, 2015, p. 9), or the fear of having another attack.

The biological mechanisms in panic attacks are similar to any anxiety disorder, a triggering event activates your primary stress response of fight-or-flight. With panic, however, onset is sudden and extreme. It is as though your entire emotional system just blew up. The physical sensations are real and terrifying. Your thoughts typically involve terror and death. And your central emotion is fear.

In the moment, you are convinced that something is physically wrong; you believe you're in mortal danger. Faced with a life-or-death situation, your brain jumps into gear, ensuring your survival. However, the emotional upheaval is too great. Your prefrontal cortex loses control of the situation, and your amygdala takes over. You are no longer able to problem solve or rationalize what is happening. You are at the mercy of your feelings.

If you were able to think rationally in the moment, you would know that fight-or-flight responses only last for a few minutes. Oxytocin, also part of the stress response, will encourage you to reach out. However, the intensity of your emotions will cause faulty thinking. Your social connections won't be enough to overrule your irrational thoughts.

Panic attacks are terrifying. That is part of the reason we fear having them again. The cycle of attack and worry-about-attack reinforces our fear narrative. This is why it's so difficult to move past panic—the constant cycle of extreme emotions ⤳ worry ⤳ avoidance.

Take a moment and think about the last time you experienced very intense feelings using Activity 27: My Thoughts About Panic. What happened? What were your thoughts and feelings? Did you panic? Recognizing a pattern of panic is necessary if you are going to move past it.

ACTIVITY 27

MY THOUGHTS ABOUT PANIC

Directions: Think about the times you have had intense anxiety or a panic attack. Complete the chart using those experiences.

My panic is triggered by . . .	When I panic, I feel . . .
When I panic, it gets worse when I . . .	When I panic, it gets better when I . . .

Leaning Into Panic

As I mentioned before, panic attacks can feel terrifying. During the attack, every instinct inside screams "run!" And when we do, if we fight against what we're feeling, if we suppress all of our instincts and symptoms, the panic gets worse. So, what are we supposed to do?

The answer is to lean in. Surrender to your feelings, move with the wave of emotion, and give yourself the gift of time. Fight-or-flight responses are not long-lasting. Within a short period, the panic will subside. Fighting and resisting only perpetuates the problem. Researchers recommend a similar response to panic: Feel the feelings, accept your reaction, move with the wave of emotions, and wait (Bourne, 2015; Weekes, 1990). Let's examine each aspect of the response.

Acquiescing to a panic attack is not easy. Every instinct says the opposite. But when you can feel the panic and purposefully witness each moment, you communicate trust and acceptance. You tell yourself, "I can do this!" Furthermore, accepting your feelings and reactions enables you to float through them without reacting.

I often refer to this as leaning into the panic. You've probably heard the phrase "roll with the punches"—this is the same idea. Acquiesce to your body's reactions to stress and be the witness to your own actions without tensing up and fighting them. This will give you the space and time you need to calm the amygdala and bring your rational brain back online.

Leaning into panic does not mean adopting a passive position. In fact, fleeing and freezing can be as unhelpful as fighting. Instead, learn to reframe the thoughts as you have them. Use the technique in Activity 28: My Empowering Statements to support your mind as you travel through the panic.

Take a moment to complete Activity 28: My Empowering Statements. Read each of the provided symptoms (common physical sensations we may have during a panic attack). Take a moment to note what thoughts or cons you may be experiencing. Then, reframe them into empowering coping statements. Use these statements whenever you experience significant overwhelming feelings or panic.

Another way to practice leaning into panic is through mindfulness and present moment awareness. It is often said that fear lives in reference to the past and anxiety lives in anticipation of the future. Being aware of the present moment negates the impact of both.

MY EMPOWERING STATEMENTS

Directions: For each symptom of panic listed (and any that you add), list the negative thought(s) or con(s) that would be triggered. You may have more than one con. Do this for every symptom before completing the final column. After you've made the list of cons, go through each entry and reframe it using empowering statements.

Panic Symptom	Negative Thought or Mental Con(s)	Empowering Statement
Sinking feeling in stomach or abdomen	Example: "I'm going to be sick. This is really, really bad."	Example: "I'm okay. The feeling is just my body telling me I need to step up and pay attention. I can do this. I am strong."
Tightness in chest or throat		
Nausea or diarrhea		
Feeling faint		
Fear of dying		
Fear of going crazy		

Chapter 8 and 9 discuss a variety of ways to achieve present moment awareness. Use some of those strategies the next time you experience a panic attack. Try noticing everything about your response to panic, from your physical response, to your feelings, to your thoughts. Guard against taking action as you witness these or against initiating new fear and anxiety by engaging in negative self-talk ("I'm so stupid") or toxic errors of thinking ("I must be dying if I feel like this"). Simply notice without judgment or attachment.

Your Fear Narrative

Throughout this book, I have spoken about the role of fear and your fear story. Fear is a primal emotion. Like your stress response, the role of fear is to alert you to danger. Your fear narrative is the story that exists inside and is created by your experiences with fear. It's what you tell yourself when you panic, a collection of thoughts, cognitive errors, and cons all rooted in your fear.

Your fear narrative is sometimes referred to as your shadow self or your invisible suitcase. You carry this narrative with you throughout your life. It influences the choices you make and the ways you utilize your stress responses.

Fear always serves the mind, working to ensure your survival. However, it often functions from a false reality, triggering a threat response even when there is no sign of danger. Understanding your fear narrative is vital to the process of letting go. Fortunately, you've already practiced a variety of tools that will help you uncover the role fear has played in your life.

Take a moment and revisit Activity 18: Recognizing the Cons (p. 70). Through that exercise, you evaluated how your mental cons served you, how they kept you safe. This is part of your fear narrative. In Activity 19: My Triggers (p. 71), you identified the things that most frequently solicit your anxiety. This is also part of your experience with fear. Go back through every exercise. Read through your responses. What have you learned about your relationship with fear? How has it served you? How has it hurt you?

Now, complete Activity 29: My Fear Narrative. As you begin to recognize the role of fear, look for ways you can continue to rewrite your narrative.

ACTIVITY 29 ⇐
MY FEAR NARRATIVE

Directions: Think about everything you've learned about fear and your fear narrative. Take a moment to complete the questions below. Use your inner persona if you are struggling to answer the questions. Write your answers in the space provided or in your journal.

- What is my experience with fear? _____
  _____
  _____
  _____
  _____

- How has my fear hurt or limited me?_____
  _____
  _____
  _____
  _____

- How has my fear served me? _____
  _____
  _____
  _____
  _____

- What do I want to say to my fear? _____
  _____
  _____
  _____
  _____

An Important Note About Panic Attacks and Severe Anxiety

Dealing with severe forms of anxiety and panic often require the assistance of a mental health professional. Do not view this as a bad thing. You are not "broken" if you need help. In fact, seeking help is a positive sign of wellness. Find someone with a similar perspective on mental health, one who embraces your therapeutic goals. Activity 30: What I Want From Therapy can help you identify the important qualities you would like in a therapist, as well as your goals. Use this chart as you find help and while receiving assistance.

Once you have found a mental health professional to partner with you on your road to wellness, continue to work on those exercises in the book that support the work you are doing in therapy. Moving through anxiety and panic is a process. It takes time, dedication, and patience. But it can be accomplished. I have worked with many young women throughout my career. They have made this journey. I, too, have made this journey. I know firsthand that you can move past your unhelpful mental thoughts and let go of the pain and panic. But you need to start; you need to take the first step.

Ciara's Story

Thank you for sharing a bit of your story with me today. Let's start by understanding what you mean by panic. Can you describe a typical panic attack?

CIARA: Sure. Panic attacks are like the worst nightmare you can imagine—except it's really happening! Your heart starts to pound, your head aches, and your mind races. For me, I felt like I was going to die. Literally. My throat would close and my heart would beat so hard I wondered if my chest would crack open. The world spun away from me. Nothing made logical sense when I was in the middle of an episode. All I could think about was surviving the attack.

How long did they last?

CIARA: The initial attack would only last a few minutes. But I could never relax after an attack. I worried that it would happen again, and often that would trigger another attack. It was a rough cycle to disrupt.

ACTIVITY 30 ⇐

WHAT I WANT FROM THERAPY

Directions: Think about the qualities you want in a therapist or counselor. What values or approaches are important to you?

_____

_____

_____

_____

Take a moment to write one or two goals for therapy. Share these with you mental health professional.

Goal	Potential Barriers	Action Plan	Benefits to Completing Goal
Example: I would like to learn how to better manage my panic.	• I am resisting the "work." • I won't be honest about how frequently I panic.	• I can commit every day to doing something small that will help me. • I can keep a journal of the episodes and share it with my therapist.	• I can reduce the amount of panic I feel and have more energy to build other skills.

You mentioned that one attack would often trigger another. Were there other triggers?

CIARA: Yes and no. There were some things that consistently triggered me—lack of sleep, arguments with my mom or dad, being sick or around sick people. But even if I avoided all of that, I still experienced panic attacks, sometimes for no apparent reason. I could eat something and panic. Go to my favorite park and panic. It got to the point that just existing could throw me into a state of panic.

How did you begin to work past the attacks? When did the intensity lessen?

CIARA: I saw a therapist for my anxiety and panic attacks after the third attack. We worked to identify why I was having them and how to reduce or eliminate them. It took over a year before I had any consistent relief. Truthfully, I spent the first year on a rough rollercoaster. I'd start to get better and have fewer attacks, only to get hit with a big one when I least expected it. This would lead to the negative self-talk and behaviors that created the problem initially. It was a hard cycle to break. But eventually I did, and the attacks became fewer and fewer.

Were there particular strategies that helped?

CIARA: My therapist and I developed a "panic ladder" on one of our first visits—this was a chart of the things that frightened me, from the easiest to overcome to the hardest. She taught me a lot of coping strategies, things like deep breathing and mindfulness, and then exposed me to my fears. It was difficult at first. Even the low-level fears on my chart overwhelmed me easily. But we practiced a lot.

If you could give advice to a young woman wrestling with similar issues, what would you say?

CIARA: Hang in there. My therapist used to say that there is no failure, only opportunities for growth. I think this is true. Each time I struggled I had a chance to try the strategy again. Recovering from panic disorders takes a while. The journey is rough at times, and not always fun. But nothing feels as good as regaining control over your mind and your emotions. So, hang in there. If you try a variety of strategies and they aren't helping you, keep trying. You will eventually figure out what works. You just have to be willing to try again.

Ciara learned to manage and move past the bonds of anxiety and panic. You can too.

Life is not perfect. There will be stressful situations. We will have occasions when our responses are overly emotional. That's just part of our shared human experience. However, you can learn to regain control of your thinking before it spins too far out of control. And you can learn to prevent some panic-filled moments from occurring. The key is awareness—of your thinking, of any cognition errors, and of your ability to reframe your thoughts.

The last part of this book focuses on developing proactive habits that minimize the negative impact of stress in your life and maximize your brain's natural ability to be resilient. As you go through the various chapters and activities, consider the work you've already accomplished. Incorporate your experiences into the upcoming activities as often as possible. But first, take a look at the reflection questions below. Think about your most intense responses to anxiety and fear. Learning how you react when pushed beyond your limits will help you learn to manage your everyday reactions as well.

Do the Work

Use these reflection questions to bring you to a deeper understanding of your thoughts and feelings about the information in this chapter. Consider focusing on one or two topics every time you journal.

- What am I most afraid of when I begin to panic? Describe the fear in detail.
- What would it be like to lean into my fear? Imagine it fully.
- In what ways have my fears served me?
- What is the positive version of my fear or the positive message it gives me?
- What can I do right now to reframe my fear into a strength?

Part III

FROM SURVIVING TO THRIVING

At this point in the book, you've begun to recognize the roles stress and anxiety have played in your life. You may have also started to reframe your definitions of these emotional states, changed your responses, and moved through some of the unpleasantness that often accompanies extreme emotional upheaval. Now it's time to learn to do more than survive your stress.

Now you'll learn to thrive!

Over the next three chapters, I'll guide you through the foundational pieces of living a life free from the dysfunctional side of stress. You'll learn to discern which habits contribute to your overall physical and emotional health and which do not. You'll also begin to cultivate awareness, compassion, and relaxation habits that can infuse your life with a sense of calm. And finally, you learn to detox your mindset and embrace gratitude and joy in all aspects of life. Bringing together the science of positive neuropsychology and transformational practices, these activities have the power to positively impact your daily experiences.

As always, I'd like us to start with a brief assessment of your current lifestyle habits and mindset beliefs, found in Activity 31: My Lifestyle, My Mindset.

Understanding your current beliefs will help you assess which, if any, aspects of your mindset you'd like to enhance or change. After you complete the quiz in Activity 31, please take a moment to develop goals for this final section of the book using Activity 32: Goals for Part III.

In addition to the goals for this section, I've developed a special road-map for you to personalize that I call My Road to Release (Activity 33). As you complete each of these last chapters, take a moment to complete the corresponding part of the roadmap. This will serve as your action plan and a way to hold yourself accountable for the changes you'd like to make over time.

Thank you for journeying with me thus far. I am excited to complete this path with you.

ACTIVITY 31 ⇐
MY LIFESTYLE, MY MINDSET

Directions: Take a few minutes to consider the statements below, marking which ones are true for you, and determine your lifestyle and mindset.

♦ Eating Healthy
   a. I know how to construct a healthy and well-balanced meal.
   b. I have a variety of food options available to me in my house.
   c. I try to reduce my intake of sugar and caffeine.
   d. If I don't have access to healthy food available at home, I utilize the food options at school and make this a priority.

♦ Sleep
   a. I get at least 6 hours of sleep every night.
   b. I am tired throughout the day.
   c. I use the weekends to "catch up" on sleeping.
   d. Getting enough rest is a priority for me.

♦ Exercise
   a. I do some form of cardiovascular exercise for at least 30 minutes, three times weekly.
   b. I do some form of strength training 2–3 times weekly.
   c. I consider myself an active person.
   d. Finding time for physical activities is a priority for me.

♦ Relaxation/Mindfulness
   a. I turn off my electronics an hour before going to bed.
   b. I find myself "on edge" or anxious throughout the day.
   c. I try to meditate, pray, or do yoga at least twice a week.
   d. I actively practice mindfulness daily.

♦ Mindset
   a. I consider myself optimistic.
   b. I practice self-compassion daily.
   c. I am at least as happy as my friends.
   d. I have good friendships in my life.

♦ Miscellaneous
   a. Three activities I like to do every day for my physical or mental health are . . . (complete the sentence).
   b. I have a gratitude practice I do at least twice a week.
   c. I am around negative people or situations more than five times a week.

Note. Adapted from *The Girl Guide: Finding Your Place in a Mixed-Up World* (p. 36), by C. Fonseca, 2013, Waco, TX: Prufrock Press. Copyright 2013 by Prufrock Press. Adapted with permission.

ACTIVITY 32 ⇐

GOALS FOR PART III

Directions: Take a moment to think about the final section of *Letting Go*. Set a few goals related to developing the positive habits you need to support your efforts to release yourself from the hold of anxiety. What do you hope to accomplish as you work through Part III of *Letting Go*?

Goal	Potential Barriers	Action Plan	Benefits to Completing Goal
Example: I want to develop an optimistic mindset and experience more happiness.	• I typically view things in a negative way. • I have so much stress and anxiety, I struggle to see the positive. • I don't have time to try to be positive. • It feels like a lot of work.	• I can reframe my thoughts to a positive perspective. • I can focus on how these skills help me. • I can commit to 5–10 minutes every day to develop these skills. • I can decide that I'm worth the work.	• Viewing the world from a positive mindset will help me feel happier every day.

ACTIVITY 33 ⇐

MY ROAD TO RELEASE

Directions: Throughout the last section of the book, you will be completing a plan to continue the work you have been doing related to your anxiety. Complete the appropriate section after each chapter.

	Creating a Healthy Foundation							
Key Messages	Activities to Practice (From the Whole Book)	Goals	Barriers	Action Plan				
Example: Developing an optimistic mindset is important in helping with my anxiety.	• Jumps Toward Joy	I want to practice something from the Healthy Lifestyle chart every day.	I may get busy and decide that the work isn't important.	• Choose one activity each day. • Chart when I do the activity. • If I complete the activities at least 5/7 days, celebrate the success.				

Living Life in Every Breath	Key Messages	Activities to Practice (From the Whole Book)	Goals	Barriers	Action Plan

The Power of Perception.

Key Messages	Activities to Practice (From the Whole Book)	Goals	Barriers	Action Plan

Chapter 7

CREATING A HEALTHY FOUNDATION

What does it mean to live a life in balance? What are the important, high leverage things you can do daily to increase your personal resilience and improve your stress reactions? In this chapter, we will explore these questions and more.

I have worked with many girls who struggle to find balance in high school and college. Between school, work, a job, extracurricular activities, and family expectations, it is easy to forget to take care of yourself. Things don't improve once you are out of school. Women at all stages of life struggle with balancing their personal needs with the demands of work and within the family.

What is the cost for the lack of balance? For most, it involves a loss of coping strategies, increased emotional upheaval, and a reduced sense of "flourishing." In other words, you will not thrive when you are not engaging in appropriate self-care.

Over the next several pages, you will explore your personal costs for living an unbalanced life. You will also begin to discover what aspects of healthy living are most criti-

cal for you, and plan out ways to create a life based on your healthy habit nonnegotiables.

You may be tempted to skip over this chapter or parts of this chapter. I urge you to reconsider. Researchers have found significant links between our daily lifestyle choices and our ability to cope with life's stressors (Bourne, 2015). Take the time to do the exercises and the journaling questions at the end. You may discover something new about yourself!

Seeking Balance

Living a life in balance means engaging in daily practices that enhance, rather than diminish, your everyday functioning. Food, sleep patterns, exercise, relaxation, mindset, and relationships all factor into our overall balance. It is important to recognize how each of these aspects of daily living influence your thoughts and feelings.

⇥ Nutrition

Researchers are only now beginning to fully understand the mind-body connection, finding connections between what we eat and how we feel. Some foods, including berries, avocados, and dark chocolate, contribute to feelings of calm, while others, including refined sugars and flours, alcohol, and foods high in salt, increase your stress response and aggravate anxiety.

One item in particular is thought to significantly (and negatively) impact anxiety—caffeine. Found in many types of tea, coffee, chocolate, candy, and soda, caffeine stimulates your nervous system, causing an arousal of your stress response (Bourne, 2015). If you already struggle to maintain emotional balance, consuming high amounts of caffeine will most certainly aggravate it.

Other foods and substances can stress your body as well. Salt, added hormones, and GMOs all impact the body by placing it under increased stress—which is not good if you are working hard to break free of a negative stress response cycle.

As you work to balance your daily lifestyle choices, consider the role of food in your life. Eating healthy will make it easier to maintain emotional well-being.

➤➤ Sleep

Balanced lifestyle choices are not limited to food. Researchers also agree that sleep is vital to a healthy way of life. Have you ever wondered why it's so hard to concentrate when you are tired? Or why you feel more on edge and prone to argue with friends when you haven't had enough sleep? The answer lies in the role sleep plays in brain development. Sleep is involved in more than five major brain processes, including memory, attention, learning, and emotional processing (Tarokh, Saletin, & Carskadon, 2016). And although getting an insufficient amount of sleep is not uncommon for women, especially teens, there is a cost to pay. Recent research has indicated that poor sleep, either in terms of the quantity (number of hours you sleep) or the quality (how much deep sleep is obtained), can result in an increase in mental health concerns, including anxiety, depression, and panic (Paruthi et al., 2016). That's right, sleep can absolutely impact your ability to manage your anxiety.

But how much sleep do you actually need? Most researchers recommend between 8 and 10 hours nightly for girls between the ages of 13 and 18 (Paruthi et al., 2016). I know, you are likely getting far less than that amount, especially during the school week. Although it is definitely difficult to obtain adequate sleep, there are a few things you can do, including developing a sleep routine with consistent sleep and wake times, turning off your electronics (including your phone), and making the amount and quality of sleep you get a priority.

It is easy to neglect the importance of sleep to your functioning at school, but consider this. Your brain actually requires rest to efficiently process information. Reducing the amount of sleep you get just to study longer for a test or complete the last bit of homework may prove to be ineffective in the long run, especially if the price is a poor memory and increased anxiety.

➤➤ Exercise

In addition to healthy choices around food and sleep, appropriate exercise is critical to a healthy lifestyle. Researchers have linked moderate exercise (defined as 30 minutes of brisk walking or running 3–5 times each week) to a reduction in stress and anxiety symptoms (Powers, Asmundson, & Smits, 2015). Have you ever heard of the term *runner's high*? Aerobic exercise, including walking, running, swimming, and dancing, increases the brain's production of feel-good chemicals called endorphins. Although exercise increases certain neurotransmitters, it significantly reduces negative stress hormones including cortisol and adrenaline. Also, regular exercise can improve brain processes including cognition and emotional processing and help to regulate sleep.

Sadly, most teens are becoming less and less active. Sedentary activities like reading, playing video games, watching TV, and playing on smartphones have resulted in significant declines in physical exercise. As you balance out the areas of nutrition and sleep, consider the amount of exercise you get every day. Look for opportunities to take a brisk walk, dance with friends, or participate in a sport. Not only will you improve your brain and body's response to stress and anxiety, but you may also have fun!

➺ Relaxation

Just as sleep is essential to brain development, so is relaxation. Chapter 8 focuses heavily on mindfulness and relaxation. For now, I want you to consider the role relaxation and mindfulness have in your life. Do you regularly engage in activities that relax your mind and body? What are they? Do you remember to give yourself a relaxing "brain break" during periods of study and homework?

Relaxation is essential to a healthy lifestyle. Researchers have found that strategies that calm your mind and body reduce the harmful impact of stress hormones, relax the activation of your fight-or-flight response, and improve mental focus. Even something as small as a single guided relaxation module on a relaxation app can reduce the negative impact of stress and anxiety (Unger, Busse, & Yim, 2017).

➺ Mindset

Happiness, optimism, and gratitude—these are more than platitudes offered up by popular psychologists. Researchers in these areas have demonstrated a strong connection between our state of mind and our ability to handle stressful situations (McGonigal, 2015). Chapter 9 provides several specific strategies for cultivating a mindset that fosters a strong well-being. For now, consider the role mindset currently plays in your everyday functioning. Do you actively engage in activities that promote your happiness? Are you generally optimistic about your future? Do you regularly give thanks for the good things in your life? The answers to these questions can help you determine which areas you may need to develop as you begin to cultivate a well-balanced life.

Table 5, Features of a Healthy Lifestyle, summarizes many of the aspects of healthy living I've outlined here. You can use the chart in Activity 34: Daily Lifestyle Choices, along with the quiz in Activity 31: My Lifestyle, My Mindset, as a starting point to develop your specific lifestyle plan. As you work through each section, observe your inner thoughts and feelings. Are there specific themes that emerge? Are some ideas and strategies more important than others?

For me, daily journaling is as necessary as eating healthy and sleeping. Through my journaling, I am able to witness my thoughts and feelings, making adjustments as needed. In fact, daily journaling is so important to me, I consider it one of my nonnegotiable, must-dos every day.

As you review your completed lifestyle worksheet, see if you can identify a few of your most important aspects of healthy living. For some of you, it may be exercise or yoga. Others may find pleasure reading a must-do item. It doesn't matter which specific things resonate most with you, only that you begin to identify the things you need to stay in balance.

Emotional Balance

Speaking of balance, healthy habits also extend into emotional well-being. Researchers consider emotional awareness the recognition of one's emotional state and the beginnings of emotional regulation, citing it as a needed skill in the recovery of severe anxiety and depression (Kranzler et al., 2016). Learning to recognize, label, and monitor your feelings, much as you have done throughout the exercises in this book, is key to your overall emotional wellness. Through the act of witnessing and other skills, you are able to not only see when your feelings and thoughts are askew, but also begin to change your response. Each of the exercises you've completed to date have helped to improve this skill.

But emotional balance includes more than regulation. It also includes understanding what you *want* to feel in a variety of situations.

Consider this example: You are getting ready to attend a new school. Although you are excited, you are also worried that you may not like the school or the other students. You fear they may not accept you. These feelings are all rooted in your past experiences, responses to stress and anxiety, and anticipatory stress.

TABLE 5
Features of a Healthy Lifestyle

Nutrition	*Sleep*	*Exercise*
• Eat balanced meals, including calming foods like avocados and berries. • Avoid refined sugar and caffeine as much as possible. • Avoid GMOs and added hormones in your food.	• Aim for 8–10 hours of sleep nightly. • Develop a sleep ritual to help you fall asleep. • It's normal to wake during the night, as long as you can easily return to sleep. • Track your sleep habits using an app or journal.	• Aim for 30 minutes of aerobic activity 3–5 times a week. • Track steps or other activities daily using a step counter, app, or Fitbit. • Consider movement breaks during periods of homework or as a study break. • Vary exercise activity and exercise with friends.
Relaxation	*Mindset*	*Other*
• Add mindfulness activities to increase periods of relaxation and calm. • Use brain breaks to relax in between study sessions. • Practice breathing exercises to enhance feelings of calm.	• Focus on developing a growth mindset. • Practice happiness and optimism frequently. • Look for opportunities to smile and play. • Include gratitude in your weekly habits. • Track your mindset in your journal.	• Use this space to add your own things that help foster a healthy lifestyle:

You are aware of both your feelings and why you have them. You've reframed negative self-talk into empowering statements and chosen an adaptive stress mindset. Still, your worries linger.

What if you could view the situation through a slightly different lens? Would you possibly find a different perspective? I think you might.

If you focused not on what you were currently feeling about the situation (apprehension, excitement, and worry) and instead determined what you wanted to feel (belonging, gratitude for your new friendship opportunities, and joy), you would be able to tailor your empowering statements

DAILY LIFESTYLE CHOICES

Directions: Review the quiz, My Lifestyle, My Mindset. Using that information, complete the worksheet below.

Area of Focus	Reflections	Action Plan	High Importance Items
Relaxation/ mindfulness	Example: I don't think about this enough. I want to add more mindfulness and relaxation.	• Practice mindful minutes in which I focus on my breathing every day. • Use a journal every day. • Turn off phone every night by 10 (before I go to bed).	• Journaling

toward moving you in the direction of your desired feelings. Like Jack Sparrow's special compass that guides you to the thing you want most, you could create your desired feelings by directing your thoughts to yield a sense of belonging, gratitude, and joy. As those emotions take hold, you will act in a way that reflects your inner reality, shaping the world around you.

In Activity 35: What Do I Desire?, identify the positive feelings you want to have in your life. Don't worry about how many you identify, just create a bank of positive emotions. Then list a variety of activities you engage in regularly. For each event or activity, write the emotion you'd like to feel. Then write one thing you can do to move you in the direction of that feeling.

As you focus on what you want to feel and begin to alter your thoughts and actions to help achieve that goal, you will gain more autonomy over your life. Additionally, you will find more emotional regulation and balance, all contributing to a more adaptive stress mindset.

Another way to achieve emotional balance and enhance your well-being is through the recognition and use of your personal strengths. Positive psychology researchers have determined that regularly using your strengths throughout your life increases your sense of well-being and happiness, and works as a buffer against stress, anxiety, and depression (Duan & Bu, 2017; Morimoto, Takahashi, & Namiki, 2015). Furthermore, when you are able to not only recognize your strengths in a variety of situations, but also intentionally use your strengths in new ways for as little as a week, you can strengthen your emotional well-being, increase happiness, and decrease depression for 3 months or more (Duan & Bu, 2017; Mongrain & Anselmo-Matthews, 2012).

The first step in using your strengths is to identify your personal character strength profile. Activity 36: Understanding My Strengths will guide you through developing a strengths profile. Start by taking the free strengths survey from the VIA Institute of Character Development (http://www.viacharacter.org/www/Character-Strengths-Survey) and watch the short video, "The Science of Character" (https://youtu.be/U3nT2KDAGOc). After you've determined your strength profile, use Activity 36 to highlight your strengths and discover how you currently use them. You will then develop a plan to use your strengths in new ways.

As you move toward balance in your life through the development of healthy lifestyle choices and recognition of your strengths, what are you feeling? Does the focus on these foundational skills begin to shift your thinking? Are you feeling more empowered? These are just a few of the changes that may happen as you begin this work.

ACTIVITY 35 ⇐

WHAT DO I DESIRE?

Part 1

Directions: Read each "desire" word. Circle those that best represent the values and feelings you want in your life.

Acceptance	Accomplishment	Acknowledgment	Affection	Alive
Amazed	Awe	Appreciation	Balance	Boldness
Brave	Calm	Capable	Cheerful	Comfortable
Content	Courageous	Creative	Decisive	Determined
Eager	Elated	Elevated	Empowered	Encouraged
Excited	Fabulous	Friendship	Freedom	Fulfillment
Generous	Grateful	Grace	Grounded	Happy
Hopeful	Important	Innovative	Invigorated	Joyful
Kindness	Love	Magical	Nurtured	Optimistic
Powerful	Refreshed	Satisfied	Strong	Treasured
Understood	Vulnerable	Whole		

Part 2

Directions: List the everyday activities you regularly engage in. For each activity, choose one or two of the above feelings. Pick those things you want to feel when engaged in the activity.

Activity	Value
Example: Going to lunch with friends	*Friendship, appreciation, love*

ACTIVITY 36 ⇐

UNDERSTANDING MY STRENGTHS

Directions: Take the VIA Character Strengths survey (http://www.viacharacter.org/www/Character-Strengths-Survey) and watch the video, "The Science of Character" (https://youtu.be/U3nT2KDAGOc). Look up your top five strengths on the VIA Institute website. Using information from the website and your survey, complete this worksheet.

Top 5 Strengths (From VIA Survey)	Ways I Currently Demonstrate the Strength	Ways I Will Develop the Strength Even More (Including Movies or Books and Activities)
Example: Creativity	I show creativity in how I approach problems or write stories.	I will watch the movie A Beautiful Mind and start writing down stories, poetry, or even just my ideas every day.

The Cost of Change

It takes more effort to live a life of balance initially, especially if you need to establish a few habits from scratch. Some of you may wonder if it is worth it—if creating new, healthier habits is worth the work it is going to take to achieve. In fact, some of you may wonder if letting go and releasing your experience with anxiety is worth it at all. The truth is, you are the only one who can answer that question. Only you know the cost of continuing to live as you do with your stress and anxiety. Only you know if your lifestyle choices are hurting or helping you.

What I can tell you from personal experience is this: There are few greater gifts you can give yourself than a life in full balance. Balance enables the brain to communicate effectively and promote adaptation and resilience. Balance enables you to understand, recognize, and direct your thoughts and emotions. And balance allows you to live the life you desire, one that is filled with passion and purpose.

There are a few things, however, that balance does not mean. A balanced life doesn't mean you will never feel emotional upheaval. I guarantee that you will. Balance doesn't mean you will never feel anxiety or panic. If you are living a full life, I promise you you'll feel those things as well. And a balanced life doesn't mean you will never experience hardship. That is pretty much a guarantee, too.

What a balanced life ensures is that when those things happen, you will be prepared to meet the challenge head on. You will know how to choose the most appropriate response to the situation and you will know which strengths to tap into and how.

Finding the motivation to make the changes, even when you understand why it is important, can still be difficult. That is when a basic pros/cons list and a cost-analysis comes in to play.

No, you didn't leap into an economics or consumer math class suddenly. But many of the principals of social economics can prove helpful to find and increase the motivation necessary to change.

For this exercise, take a look at Activity 37: The Cost of Stagnancy. Take a few minutes and complete the activity. As you reflect on your answer, consider the price you will pay if you do nothing. Are you willing to pay this? How about the cost of change? Is it manageable?

Making decisions from the position of a cost analysis can help take the fear out of the task. Sometimes that is all we need in order to muster up the courage to act.

ACTIVITY 37 ⋠

THE COST OF STAGNANCY

Directions: Determine what behavior/thought you want to change. Write it down.

_____

_____

_____

Answer the following questions about the change listed above.

What is the "price" I am currently paying to stay with this behavior (i.e., if the behavior is my negative thinking, the price I currently pay are my feelings of anxiety that come every day)? _____

_____

_____

What is the "price" I will pay if I change the behavior (i.e., if I work to reframe my negative thinking, I would pay the price of having to complete the worksheets and think about my behavior a lot)? _____

_____

_____

Is this "price" worth it to change my behavior? _____

_____

_____

Think about the pros (good things, benefits) and cons (bad things, costs) of changing the behavior listed above. Complete the chart with the things you've identified.

Pros	Cons

Speaking of courage, I would be remiss if I left out any talk of courage when we are discussing change and balance. All shifts, forward or back, require an act of courage. As I mentioned earlier, humans do not like to change, even when the change will enhance their lives. Making the decision to act, and continuing to act even when your body and mind are resisting, is brave. Fortunately, you are wiser than you realize, and your stress response will give you the courage you need.

Remember our previous conversation about stress and the hormone oxytocin? Not only does this hormone increase social connections and protect your body in times of stress, but it also decreases your fear resistance, enabling small acts of courage.

Benjamin Mee's 2008 book, *We Bought a Zoo*, and the movie by the same name have one of my all-time favorite courage quotes. In the scene, Ben tells his son that sometimes all anyone needs is "20 seconds of insane courage" (Crowe, 2011; Mee, 2008) to change his or her life. The movie then goes on to show a scene in which the main character musters up the courage to talk to his future wife. Imagine what must be going on inside his mind: He sees the girl, triggering a strong emotional response. He wants to talk with her, but he feels afraid, concerned he may be humiliated. His stress response initiates, urging him to act. As his fear grows, his instinct tells him to run. Fortunately, the oxytocin compels him to reach out, suppressing some of his fear in the process. Bam! Courage. He talks to the girl, and the rest is book/movie magic.

Living a balanced life, deciding to build new ways of interacting with your stress and the world, staying on course even when it's hard—these are acts of "embarrassing bravery." Take the time to acknowledge every moment, every attempt you have made in your journey to change your experiences of stress and anxiety. If you have a result you didn't expect or want, try again. Each opportunity has the potential to move you toward your desires. Take advantage of them all.

In Activity 38: Insane Courage, I want you to reflect on the scene I mentioned above. Watch the movie clip and answer the questions on the worksheet. Then imagine your own opportunities to experience 20 seconds of insane courage. What would you do with that kind of courage? How would your life change?

Finding the motivation and courage to change isn't easy. But the payoff is more than worth it. You are worth it!

ACTIVITY 38 ⇐

INSANE COURAGE

Directions: Watch two clips from the movie *We Bought a Zoo* (https://youtu.be/ZmM FIganRQY and https://youtu.be/mqE-yAfYAhw).

• What strengths does the character Benjamin Mee demonstrate in the scene?

_____

_____

_____

♦ How does his stress response help him?

_____

_____

_____

Think about what you would do with 20 seconds of courage. Dream big! In your journal or in the space provided, explain what you would do with 20 seconds of courage.

_____

_____

_____

_____

_____

What strengths would you use to make the above happen?

_____

_____

_____

_____

I really can't remember a time when I didn't deal with anxiety. As a young child, I struggled with separation anxiety. In elementary school and middle school, my parents said I had performance anxiety. In college, I was diagnosed with generalized anxiety disorder and panic. So, I guess you can say anxiety has always been part of my life.

I've tried many different ways to mitigate the anxiety: therapy (individual and group), medication, ignoring it completely. You name it, I've probably tried it. Most things worked for a little while, giving me periods of respite between the storms of my emotions. But nothing worked longer than a few weeks or months.

I thought I was just destined to be anxious, that I would always deal with underlying feelings of panic. Calm was constantly elusive to me, and I eventually stopped believing anything would be very different.

That changed over the past 3 years.

A friend of mine recognized my anxiety one day at work. We both worked for the same advertising firm. She noticed how frequently I went to the restroom when a big project was due. Or how often I would text someone or "disappear" during heightened stress. One day, she asked me if I ever felt anxiety. I laughed and told her about my past. She just smiled.

It turned out that she had a similar story. She found relief with a local therapist. Tired of feeling stuck in my anxiety, I decided to try one last time. I am so thankful I did.

The process was similar to the other therapeutic experiences I've had: We get to know each other and set goals, I get homework to work on, and we process through it together in follow-up visits. Except this time, there was another piece. This therapist asked me to make an action plan—a roadmap to guide me to my recovery. On the map, I listed the specific strategies that helped me. I also had journal sections to explore the role the anxiety had in my life, the benefits I felt from it, and my current self-talk.

The roadmap helped a lot. By constantly writing and revising my plan, I was able to better integrate some of the strategies into my everyday functioning. Before, I only used the strategies sparingly, and typically when I didn't really need them. Whenever a big triggering event happened, I resorted to old ways of responding because I could never remember the new strategies. With my plan, I kept the strategies with me. I could refer to them any time I needed to.

Now, a few years later, most of my best strategies are habits. I don't need to look at my plan, although I continue to keep it with me and reflect on it often. I don't use the old habits very much now, and when I do, I can quickly switch my thinking. I like to think that I have retrained my brain!

Throughout this chapter, you learned how your everyday lifestyle choices impact your overall functioning and ability to cope with stress and anxiety. The greater your emotional response during periods of stress, the more important it is to establish healthy lifestyle habits. As you complete the reflection questions below and begin to develop your Road to Release action plan (p. 109), consider your previous discoveries about how you currently manage emotional upheaval. The more honest you can be with yourself as you develop your plan, the more relief you will find as you do the work.

Do the Work

Use the questions below to bring you to a deeper understanding of your thoughts and feelings about the information in this chapter. Consider focusing on one or two topics every time you journal.

- What lifestyle choices contribute to the incorrect messages or cons that I engage in?
- What would happen if I adopted new lifestyle choices that enhanced my daily functioning and allowed me to discern my old messages more readily?
- What are the nonnegotiables I need to commit to right now?
- What thoughts come up when I consider making these changes? Do any barriers surface? What are they?
- What can I do right now to make lifestyle changes that will enable me to move toward my goals?

In addition to journaling, please take a moment to revisit your Road to Release worksheet in Activity 33. Complete the first section about your daily lifestyle habits and personal strengths profile. Be sure to commit to a few things from the roadmap each week—this will lead to sustainable change.

Chapter 8

LIFE IN EVERY BREATH

"Life in every breath," is part of a quote from *The Last Samurai*, one of my favorite movies (Zwick, 2003). The speaker is conveying the need to find life, or purpose, in every action, every moment, every breath—conscious living. It is a concept that addresses the need to cultivate present moment awareness, or mindfulness, as a way of increasing one's focus and quieting the incessant chatter that often fills our minds. Developing this practice enables us to not only reach a deeper state of calm within our lives, but also improve our mental functioning and resilience (Bamber & Schneider, 2016).

Some of my first experiences with conscious living came in college. I took several philosophy courses as part of my program. One class introduced me to Quaker philosophy and ideals. I wasn't completely unfamiliar with the Quaker way of life—my mother had exposed me to many religious practices since I was very young, including Quakerism. But this class enabled me to delve more deeply into their ideals. In short, Quakers believe in an intensely personal relationship with the divine. They also believe that the outward life should reflect the inner experience with divinity (Robinson, 2009). In other words, we should experience the divine in every breath, every act. Something as simple as gardening or doing laundry is an opportunity to commune with the divine.

Although I am not advocating for the Quaker or any other particular religious tradition, I am suggesting that conscious living, or being aware of every moment and finding opportunities for growth and learning in all things, is a worthy goal. In this chapter, you will begin to experience deeper awareness by learning and practicing skills in mindfulness, relaxation, and conscious awareness. In developing these skills, you increase your tolerance for adverse stress and build your resilience. You will begin to learn how to bring yourself into a relaxed state quickly and use these strategies when your anxiety hits. In this way, the skills learned in this chapter can become part of the arsenal of tools you'll use to manage and move through the adverse effects of stress and anxiety.

Present Moment Awareness

Present moment awareness, or mindfulness as it is more often called, refers to the practice of slowing down and paying attention to moment-to-moment life. It is the art of being aware of your awareness in the present moment and without judgment (Biegel, 2009). Mindfulness enables you to not only witness your inner and outer worlds, but regulate your actions through intentional choice as well.

Throughout the book, you have completed exercises focused on observing your behavior. Activity 15: Witnessing, Activity 16: A Day in the Life, Activity 18: Recognizing the Cons, and others have begun to cultivate your present moment awareness. We will refine the skill more in this chapter. The practice of mindfulness involves several core components: focused attention and awareness, lack of judgment, and response suppression. In other words, mindfulness teaches you to be aware of every moment from a place of surrender that's free of judgment. It is similar to the act of leaning into panic that we discussed in Chapter 5.

Researchers have found those who practice mindfulness increase their emotional and cognitive flexibility and reduce their negative episodes of stress and anxiety (Bamber & Schneider, 2016). This makes sense to me. The more you are aware of the present moment, the more you can lean into panic and surrender, and the more you can witness without attachment, the more you are able to see the inner workings of your mind and make necessary adjustments to faulty thinking patterns and overwhelming emotions.

The practice of present moment awareness will do even more. By living in the present moment, you are able to free yourself of stress from the past and worry for the future. I previously said that fear and anxiety do not "live" in the present moment as much as they are rooted in past and future thinking. Practicing your awareness of the present enables you to free yourself from the incessant worry and rumination we often engage in, thereby decreasing the activation of your stress responses.

Practicing the art of mindfulness begins with learning to be aware. As I mentioned previously, Activity 15: Witnessing from Chapter 4 is one way to learn that skill. Here is another: Take a moment to close your eyes and notice your breath. How does it feel when you inhale deeply? Do you notice any specific sensation or scent? Place your hand on your stomach and abdomen. What does your body do as you draw breath? By paying close attention to your breathing, you are strengthening your mindfulness muscles.

Mindfulness can be done with myriad activities, from eating, to walking, to typical mundane tasks. Activity 39: Mindfulness Practice highlights a few of these things. Pick one or two items every day and tune your focus to what you are doing. You don't need to do it for long; a few minutes is sufficient. The point is to improve the act of being aware of awareness.

Combining this activity with Activity 15: Witnessing will help you develop a strong sense of present moment awareness that you can draw on whenever you are experiencing periods of stress and anxiety.

It is not unusual for your thoughts to invade your efforts at being mindful. Our brain is always at work. Mental cons, negative self-talk, and random narration about the world will often filter in and out of your conscious awareness. It is important not to make judgments when this occurs. Simply allow the thought to float in and out of your awareness. Attaching value to the idea by paying attention to it or responding in any way reinforces negative thought patterns and will often trigger additional cons or your fear narrative.

Another way mindfulness practices help overall functioning is through the awareness of the mind-body connection. Present moment awareness allows you to recognize where stress "lives" in your body. Often, a physical sensation is the first indication you consciously have of your stress response. Learning to fine-tune your awareness of your physical self can allow you to recognize your stress response early and reduce the emotional upheaval.

Let me give you a little example. I once worked with a student who experienced powerful emotions related to her giftedness and emotional intensity. She was often unaware of her internal states of anxiety and stress

ACTIVITY 39 ⇐

MINDFULNESS PRACTICE

Directions: Consider the following list of mindfulness activities. Pick one or two to try each week. As you practice the activity (i.e., mindful walking), focus your thoughts only on the activity. Notice everything you can about that activity (i.e., the way your body feels when your feet take steps, how your breathing changes as you walk faster or slower). You will notice random thoughts enter you mind. That is fine. Just let the thoughts float away and refocus on the activity you are doing.

◆ Walking	◆ Eating	◆ Driving
◆ Brushing your teeth	◆ Doing the dishes	◆ Drawing
◆ Shopping	◆ Doing homework	◆ Getting out of bed
◆ Journaling	◆ Gardening	◆ Laundry
◆ Getting dressed	◆ Dancing	◆ Walking to class
◆ Playing a sport	◆ Reading	◆ Exercising

or how her environment could trigger emotional upheaval. This resulted in extremely explosive behavior that seemed to come from nowhere.

As we worked together, I began to teach her to mindfully pay attention to her body throughout the day. I asked her to look for the earliest physical indications of stress or anxiety, similar to the exercises you did on witnessing your stress response. Through our work, she discovered that long before she explodes, she yawns and her palms itch. Every time her anxiety increased, she experienced these two physical sensations. They were the initial outward signs of distress.

Mindfulness allowed her to see this cycle. By observing her body, she could isolate her unique experience with stress. The information helped her cultivate new responses and utilize relaxation strategies before the extreme behaviors took hold.

As her ability to manage her behaviors improved, mindfulness and witnessing also enabled her to "hear" the internal messages and eventually change the thoughts and feelings behind her behavior. Awareness was the key to her growth.

I want to give you one more activity before we learn about the art of relaxation. Over the next week, practice mindfulness in all areas of your life: breathing, walking, eating, doing homework, being with friends. Notice your behavior and try to anchor yourself into the present moment. Chronicle the activities you attempt and how you feel. What did you discover? In what ways did your present moment awareness help with your experiences with stress and anxiety? Jot your thoughts on the worksheet in Activity 40: Daily Mindfulness or in your journal.

DAILY MINDFULNESS

Directions: Keep track of the mindfulness activities you try. List each one on the worksheet. Complete the rest of the worksheet.

Activity	How Did It Make You Feel?	Would You Try It Again?

The Art of Relaxation

Cultivating the art of mindfulness goes hand in hand with relaxation. As you learn to focus attention on the present moment without judgment or response, you also begin to learn how to relax. Mindful breathing, mindful meditations, and mindful body exercises all focus on relaxing the physical and mental bodies as you draw attention to the present moment. More importantly, learning to relax counteracts anxiety. Just as anxiety doesn't live within the present moment, neither does it live within a state of calm. Learning to relax in any given situation is vital to the release of anxious responses.

Did you know that many people hold their breath in response to stress? It's true and something I see all the time in school settings, especially during exams. However, holding your breath will cause tension in your body—the exact opposite of what you need when you are already experiencing a stressful response. Learning to take full, deep breaths is vital.

Try this: Close your eyes and imagine a stressful situation, one in which you generally feel anxiety. Try to visualize everything you can about that scenario until you feel your mental or physical states response. Does your body begin to tense? How about your mind? Are your thoughts starting to race?

Now, take a slow, deep breath, inhaling through your nose and exhaling through your mouth. Breathe slowly. It should feel like you are smelling a flower when you inhale, and blowing bubbles when you exhale. Using a breath count can help ensure that you are breathing slowly. Using the flower and bubbles analogy above, smell the flower (inhale) for a count of 3 (1-and-2-and-3). Hold it briefly for a count of 4 (1-and-2-and-3-and-4). Blow bubbles (exhale) for a count of 5 (1-and-2-and-3-and-4-and-5). What happened? Did you feel your body's tension begin to release? Did your mind start to settle? My guess is both things occurred. By focusing on your breath, and making certain you are slow and deliberate with each inhalation and exhalation, you are allowing your body to ease into the reality of the present moment. This kind of a relaxation exercise works because it brings you into present moment awareness, provides your cells and brain with oxygen, and stimulates your vagus nerve, an element of your nervous system that releases your fight-or-flight response and increases your state of calm. See, breathing really works!

Sometimes it is hard to breathe deeply when you are anxious. Your mind spins, you are not mindful, and you take shallow, quick breaths that resemble hyperventilation. Needless to say, you do not achieve calm during this activity. In fact, you are likely becoming more stressed.

I developed a technique called "Breathing Colors" to help with this exact thing. Designed first for *Emotional Intensity in Gifted Students* (Fonseca, 2016), Breathing Colors introduces a specific visualization for deep breathing as a way to help you learn how to breathe into your full body (see Activity 41). Start by closing your eyes. Picture a color you associate with being calm. For me, it's a beautiful ocean blue. Take a full, deep breath using the counting technique described earlier. Imagine your calming color filling your entire body. Picture the color as it expands through your chest, down to your torso, and through your limbs. When you exhale, imagine a color you associate with your anxiety (for me, that color is a muddy, brownish red), and picture it leaving your body through your mouth. Try to expel all of your breath. Repeat this process until you are exhaling the same color that you inhale.

Breathing exercises like "Breathing Colors" and others are effective ways to quickly anchor yourself in the present and release tension in your body and mind. But breathing isn't the only tool in your arsenal to relax. Learning to differentiate between tension and relaxation in your muscles can also be a powerful tool (Zucker, 2017).

Called Progressive Muscle Relaxation or Tense-and-Release, this strategy accomplishes two things: It helps you learn the difference in the feeling of tension versus relaxation, and it physically releases tension carried in your body.

Tense-and-release is simply the process of systematically tightening various muscle groups for a short period of time (5–10 seconds), followed by a release of those same muscles for another 5–10 seconds. Combining this technique with mindfulness helps you focus on the sensation of your muscles as they move from tension to relaxation. This, in turn, allows you to develop a mental script for the feelings, something to look for and assess later when you may be feeling anxiety. Try the tense-and-release strategy whenever you feel tension in your body. The specific instructions on Activity 42: Relax: Body and Mind can be used alone or with a friend to create a physical and mental sense of calm within a few minutes.

Additional strategies for relaxation can include mental imagery vacations, yoga, and mindfulness meditations. Even some of your daily lifestyle choices like journaling and exercise can contribute to your ability to recognize when you are tense and help you shift into a feeling of relaxation. The

ACTIVITY 41 ⇐

BREATHING COLORS

1. Close your eyes.
2. Picture a calming color.
3. Take a deep breath and inhale the color. Imagine it filling every part of your body.
4. Picture your stress, worries, and anxiety as a color.
5. Exhale and picture the stressful color leaving your body.
6. Repeat until the calm color is the only color you visualize in both inhalation and exhalations.
7. When you are calm, open your eyes.

ACTIVITY 42 ⇐

RELAX: BODY AND MIND

1. Sit in a chair or on the floor, with your spine straight but relaxed and your eyes closed.
2. As you take a slow, deep breath, focus your attention on your toes.
3. Scrunch your toes as tightly as you can.
4. Hold the position and your breath for a count of 4: 1-and-2-and-3-and-4.
5. Release your toes and slowly exhale your breath.
6. Repeat the above sequence with each muscle group listed below:
   - Calf muscles
   - Thighs and bottom
   - Abdomen and stomach
   - Fingers
   - Arms
   - Shoulders
   - Neck

7. After completing the sequence for each muscle group, take three deep, slow breaths. Focus only on your breathing.
8. When you are ready, open your eyes.

key is to practice several of these strategies until you can easily shift into them whenever the need arises.

Activity 43: Breathe and Relax highlights several strategies for relaxation, complete with instructions for each strategy. Pick a few to try and practice each week. I've left a few blank spots for you to fill in with strategies you've discovered. As you practice both mindfulness and relaxation, you are laying a foundation of mental and emotional wellness that will assist you as you master the other skills we've discussed throughout the book.

I've Gotta Love Me

No conversation about establishing a healthy lifestyle is complete without taking a moment to examine self-compassion. Most of us wrestle with our opinions of self at times. As discussed throughout this book, we often engage in negative self-talk, struggling to view ourselves compassionately. This behavior can derail our progress on our Road to Release, and prevent us from changing our fear narrative.

In Chapter 2, you spent some time learning to listen to your self-talk. No doubt, it was a somewhat uncomfortable task. It's hard to acknowledge the mean words we typically use with ourselves. But it is only through this process that we can reframe our relationship with our inner persona.

Self-compassion is generally defined as the ability to understand, accept, and love ourselves. It is neither about narcissism or selfishness, nor is it about pity or indulgence. It is a genuine acceptance of ourselves.

Kristen Neff, a pioneering self-compassion researcher, emphasized three attributes of self-compassion: self-kindness, recognition of our universal humanity, and mindfulness (Neff & Davidson, 2016). Self-kindness refers to the act of being kind to the self, of creating an inner dialogue that releases negative self-talk in favor of positive attribution. The exercises you have completed around your cons and self-limiting beliefs, as well as the empowering statements, increase your self-kindness.

Universal humanity is the idea that all of us share a few things in common, including the fact that we all experience pain and fear, and all of us are flawed and imperfect. These are truths of the human condition. Developing self-compassion means recognizing that everyone has "stuff" and everyone suffers. Learning to manage your anxiety or embrace a healthy lifestyle does not inoculate you from this truth. You merely learn to handle the outcome with greater grace and compassion—for yourself and those around you.

ACTIVITY 43

BREATHE AND RELAX

Directions: Consider the following list of relaxation strategies. Which have you tried? Are there others you can think of? Commit to trying a few each week.

Activity	Brief Instructions	I've Tried? Y/N
Deep Breathing	• Inhale through your nose for a count of 3. • Hold for a count of 4. • Exhale for a count of 5.	
Breathing Colors	Follow instructions on Activity 41: Breathing Colors.	
Tense and Release	Follow the instructions on Activity 42: Relax: Body and Mind.	
Mental Imagery	• Close your eyes and picture someplace that makes you feel calm. • Picture everything about the place. Use all of your senses. • Take slow, deep breaths while completing the exercise.	
Mindfulness/ Meditation	• Similar to breathing colors, sit with eyes closed. • Breath slowly and deeply. • Focus on your breathing, or use a guided meditation and follow the instructions.	
Yoga	• Slow exercise that combines stretching and mindful breathing. You can follow a YouTube instructional video or take a class.	
Journaling	• Write down your thoughts, feelings, and actions. • Use this to help gain clarity on your thoughts or stop incessant thinking patterns.	
Reading	• Choose a favorite story and read or listen to the audiobook as a way to release your stressful thoughts.	
Listening to Music	• Pick a calming song to listen to and clear your thoughts. • Or, if you need to get out big emotions, consider a fast, driving tune and dancing.	

Self-compassion and mindfulness are intrinsically linked; as you develop one, you will develop the other. Nonjudgmental awareness and acceptance cultivated in mindfulness are the same skills required for the development of self-compassion.

You have already begun to develop mindfulness, acceptance, and self-kindness through the various activities in this book. I want to provide a few more exercises to help you continue your growth with self-compassion.

You will need to commit to doing Activity 44: Dear Me for 7 days in a row. Most researchers agree that 7 days of consistent action will build new neurological pathways and change your thinking patterns. Commit to this exercise for the time needed to make lasting change.

Begin by writing to yourself from the perspective of your best friend. Make it positive, but honest. Write similar letters for 7 days, each time to you from a trusted friend. Read each letter aloud to yourself. Even better, read it while looking in the mirror (yeah, I know—super uncomfortable!). Remember to do this every day for 7 days.

This next exercise, Activity 45: I Love Me, will likely feel uncomfortable as well. Stand in front of the mirror and stare at yourself for one minute. During this time, mindfully consider your self-talk without judgment or reproach. The odds are good you are engaging in somewhat negative self-talk, hyperfocusing on any perceived flaw.

When a minute has passed, take a few moments to say three things you love about yourself. Be sure to say these out loud. You will want to laugh—that's fine. Do the task anyway.

Repeat this task daily for a week (there's that 7-day thing again). Notice if your negative self-talk decreases as you progress through the task. If you are mindfully completing the exercise, it will. You are actively rewriting your internal script about the self.

The last task in the area of self-compassion involves your personal strengths. Review the worksheet from Chapter 7 in Activity 36: Understanding My Strengths. Using the strengths list found on the VIA Character Strength website, along with your list of personal strengths, begin to recognize how strengths are demonstrated, both by you and by others. This strategy is called *strength spotting*. Developing your abilities in this area has the potential to improve your self-compassion by tapping into all of its essential components.

Complete the worksheet in Activity 46: Spot the Strength with several personal examples, as well as examples of others' strengths. Each time to

ACTIVITY 44 ⇐

DEAR ME

Directions: Start by watching the video "Write a Love Letter to Yourself" (https://youtu.be/ojUrs28LeGM). Now, take a moment to write a love letter to yourself. Tell yourself all of the kind things you want to hear. Be sure to include specific examples of your strengths.

Dear Me,
I think you are amazing! You _____

_____

_____

_____

_____

_____

_____

_____

_____

_____

_____

_____

_____

_____

_____

_____

_____

_____

Once you've written the letter, read it aloud to yourself every day for 7 days. Keep track of your progress below.

❑ Day 1   ❑ Day 2   ❑ Day 3   ❑ Day 4   ❑ Day 5   ❑ Day 6   ❑ Day 7

ACTIVITY 45 ⇐

I LOVE ME

1. Stare at yourself in the mirror for one minute.
2. Breathe deeply as you stare at yourself.
3. If negative thoughts filter through, allow them to float by.
4. If you laugh, just refocus on staring at yourself in the mirror.
5. After one minute, say three things you love about yourself out loud.

Repeat the activity every day for 7 days, keeping track of your progress below.

☐ Day 1   ☐ Day 2   ☐ Day 3   ☐ Day 4   ☐ Day 5   ☐ Day 6   ☐ Day 7

improve your abilities in this area, you are taking action to release anxiety and move from surviving to thriving.

Activity 47: Self-Compassion Practices includes a few additional exercises that can help you as you strengthen your self-compassion skills. Try them out. The more you develop this skill, the better you will float through life's challenges.

Jenna's Story

An open letter to my parents and teachers:

You often ask me to tell you about my stress and anxiety, to explain it and ask for what I need. Fine.

I struggle with stress and anxiety. A lot. Every day. But please don't think this means that I am broken. I'm not. I have big dreams that I still want to accomplish. I have hopes for the future. I just don't know how to get there, and I need your help.

"What can I do?" you often ask. It's simple. Believe me.

Believe me when I tell you it feels like the world is caving in on me, when going to school is almost too hard to bear.

Believe me when I say the things you've taught me aren't helping.

Believe me when I cry, scream, yell, and get frustrated.

Believe me, but don't think I'm broken.

I know that I will get past what I'm feeling in this moment.

I know that I can learn more strategies from you that will help.

I know that I will eventually feel better.

At least, I hope I will.

ACTIVITY 46 ⇐
SPOT THE STRENGTH

Directions: Think about different activities you have engaged in. Write a description of the activity. Which of your strengths can you spot in that activity? Complete the task using activities of things you do as well as things your friends do.

Activity	Strengths Demonstrated
Example: I helped my mom with the chores because she was traveling out of town.	Teamwork and kindness

Watch the video "Shout It Out!" (https://youtu.be/vmkLs-P5ewg). Thinking of your strengths and your dreams, combine them and make up your own shout out. Write it out here:

_____

_____

_____

_____

_____

ACTIVITY 47 ⇐

SELF-COMPASSION PRACTICES

Directions: Consider the following list of self-compassion strategies. Which have you tried? Are there others you can think of? Commit to trying a few each week.

Activity	Guiding Questions	I Tried This Activity? Thoughts?
Setting healthy boundaries	Do you make yourself a priority? Do you set healthy boundaries with others? Why are boundaries important?	
Show compassion to others	Do you regularly show compassion to others? How?	
Treating yourself as your best friend	Do you treat yourself at least as well as you treat your best friend? Have you completed the I Love Me or Dear Me activities (Activity 44 and 45)?	
Random Acts of Kindness	Do you engage in random acts of kindness? What kind things do you do for yourself?	
Assertiveness	I know how to ask for what I need? I practice being assertive as often as I can?	

Remind me of my strengths.

Remind me of my successes.

Remind me of my dreams and hopes.

With you, I can remember me and let go of my stress. With you, I can move ahead, stronger than I am today.

With you, I can thrive.

This chapter focused on relaxation and awareness as primary tools necessary to not only manage life's stressors, but in the development of self-compassion and balance. Each activity was designed to deepen your understanding of your strengths and weaknesses in these areas, as well as arm you with the tools needed to cope with other stressors as they arrive. The more you practice each of these skills, the better equipped you are to handle the setbacks that come with life. We will never outrun or escape life's ups and downs. But as you increase your brain's integration and coping skills, as well as learn to manage your emotional states, the less significant an impact these ups and downs will have on your life. You will learn to flow with the current, instead of fighting against it.

Review the reflection questions below and take a moment to answer them. The greater your awareness of the strategies to help you relax, become more mindful, and demonstrate self-compassion, the more prepared you are to handle adversity.

Do the Work

Use the questions below to bring you to a deeper understanding of your thoughts and feelings about the information in this chapter.

- What do I feel when I'm asked to be aware of awareness? Are there any blocks that surface?
- What messages to I tell myself when I am quiet?
- How do I show myself compassion?
- In what ways do I practice the art of relaxation?
- What can I do right now to infuse my life with a consistent state of calm?

In addition to journaling, please take a moment to revisit your Road to Release worksheet. Complete the second section about your awareness, relaxation, and self-compassion. Be sure to commit to a few things from the roadmap each week. This is how you make the change permanent.

LETTING GO

Chapter 9

THE POWER OF PERCEPTION

My mother used to say "the only meaning ascribed to anything is the one you place there." It was her way of teaching me about perspective. She believed that if you were struggling with things in life, you can shift your thinking about it and create a new reality. Researchers agree—mindsets highly influence reality (Seligman, 2011). How you think about your stress and anxiety significantly affects the impact these things have on your overall wellness. And, as we learned in Chapter 2, the more positively you view stress and your capacity to handle it, the more adaptive stress will be for you (McGonigal, 2015).

This chapter focuses on the power your perception has to influence your reality. From influencing the way in which stress impacts your physiology, to the impact your thinking has on your internal thought processes, understanding the power of your perception is a vital component of the development of your resiliency.

Spend time on the various exercises in this chapter. Explore your attitudes about stress and anxiety, happiness and optimism. Developing your ability to shift perspective from maladaptive to adaptive, cultivating a practice of gratitude and optimism, and finding opportunities to breathe in joy will provide a solid basis for your resilience.

In Search of Happiness

Happiness—it has become a new buzzword in popular psychology. Connecting the concepts of optimism, gratitude, mindset, and perception, the pursuit of happiness has become the cornerstone of much of the positive psychology movement. And with good reason.

Researchers have demonstrated the power of perception to alter outcomes (Crum & Phillips, 2015). From the placebo effect to self-fulfilling prophesies, attitude and mindset have been demonstrated to have a significant impact on how you respond to your world. Shifting away from maladaptive thinking to more adaptive thoughts can result in improvements in everything from the impact exercise has on your health, to stress outcomes, and even your happiness.

Recent research has indicated that happiness and wellness are linked—the happier you feel, the higher the level of emotional wellness you report. This makes sense. What you feel on the inside determines how you act in the world.

In Chapter 2, you explored stress responses and your values. In Chapter 7, you explored your character strengths and the role they play in your life. Now, I'd like you to put the two together. Begin by reviewing Part 2 of Activity 7: Everyday Values. Copy those same events onto Activity 48: It's a Matter of Strengths. Using both Activity 7: Everyday Values and Activity 36: Understanding My Strengths, I want you identify the strengths each event uses. This is similar to the strength-spotting exercise in Chapter 8. Are there certain strengths you should use? Are there particular strengths you are already using? The more you understand your strengths and learn to choose which strength to utilize and how all of this aligns with your values, the happier you can be in every aspect of your life.

Many of the exercises you've completed throughout this book were designed to help you shift perspective and build happiness. From reframing your thoughts, to using empowering statements, to building self-compassion, you have learned the tools you need to increase your own feelings of satisfaction and happiness, as well as release yourself from the pull of anxiety. See Table 6 for a reminder of these.

IT'S A MATTER OF STRENGTHS

Directions: Copy the activities and values from Part 2 of Activity 7: Everyday Values. For each activity, list the strength needed for the activity. Note whether or not the strengths listed are ones you regularly demonstrate. If they are not, look for ways to enhance those strengths.

Activity	Value	Strength Needed	Is This One of the Strengths I Regularly Use?
Example: Cleaning my room	Cleanliness and organization	Teamwork	Yes

TABLE 6

Exercises to Improve Perception and Create Happiness

Below is a list of strategies and activities to improve your perception of happiness. You will have a chance to practice each strategy as you go through the book.

Skill	Activity	
Mindset	◆ The Positive Side of Stress ◆ How Stress Serves Me ◆ Normalize My Fear ◆ Prove It! ◆ Jumps Toward Joy	◆ Thank You ◆ What Do I Desire ◆ Insane Courage ◆ Dear Me ◆ I Love Me
Empowering Statements	◆ I Choose ◆ I've Got This ◆ Prove It! ◆ Director's Notes	◆ My Empowering Statements ◆ My Inner Experts
Developing Happiness	◆ Everyday Values ◆ Understanding My Strengths ◆ Spot the Strength	◆ Dear Me ◆ I Love Me ◆ Shifting Thinking

"But I haven't finished all of the exercises," you may say. Guess what? Researchers have found that even attempting to be happy is enough to begin to elevate your mood and shift your perspective (Parks & Layous, 2016). That means simply trying the exercises—basically, showing up and attempting things—is enough to begin to improve your levels of happiness. Of course, the more you intentionally work on each activity, the greater levels of improvement you will experience. But isn't it amazing to know that even thinking about change is enough to begin the process?

Increased happiness doesn't have to be an arduous task. In addition to the various exercises offered throughout the pages of this book, you can begin to experience more satisfaction in your life simply by choosing to feel more joy.

Take a moment to reflect on your progress as you've worked through the book. How has your thinking begun to change? What "shifts" have you made? Activity 49: Shifting Thinking will give you a space to consider all of the ways you've embraced happiness on this journey of letting go. Revisit these activities any time you feel like you need to reset your internal narrative. Regular evaluation will help you maintain the new happiness and wellness you are beginning to experience.

SHIFTING THOUGHTS

Directions: Review all of the activities you've completed. For each activity, indicate whether or not the exercise helped and how it made you feel.

Activity	What Did I Learn?	How Did It Make Me Feel?

The Choice Is Optimism

My mother raised me to believe that how I felt about things in life was a choice. If I didn't like the way I was feeling, I could change it. She was right. And now researchers have proven it. Analyzing the thought patterns of optimistic and pessimistic thinking has revealed that neither is fixed. Both are mindsets that can change and shift, influencing perceptions of happiness and self-satisfaction in the process (Seligman, 2011).

Martin Seligman (2011) defined optimistic thinkers as people who describe negative events as being temporary, limited, and manageable. Pessimism takes an opposite view, engaging in all-or-nothing thinking, catastrophic beliefs, and unyielding victimization. Wow, what does that sound like?

If you said "the cons," I'd agree. Recognizing the brain's cons and cognition errors, as well as adapting alternative perspectives, is all about adopting an optimistic point of view. This must be why optimism is consistently associated with reduced anxiety and improved health outcomes (Seligman, 2011).

You've already been given a variety of ways to adopt and develop an optimistic mindset. The exercises on changing responses and correcting cognition errors are all designed with optimism in mind (see Table 7 for a list of these). Additionally, reframing your negative self-talk to empowering statements naturally shifts language away from pessimism and toward an optimistic perspective.

There are times when it is tough to find your optimism, when your inner persona is fully lost in the throes of emotional turmoil. In these moments, it may be helpful to try one more activity I like to call My Inner Experts (see Activity 50). Utilizing basic tools found throughout cognitive-behavioral therapy, including the tools in Carolyn Daitch and Lissah Lorberbaum's (2016) *The Road to Calm Workbook* (a resource I mention later as a great guide for you to use), this activity allows you to call on your inner wisdom and grace as needed to navigate difficult situations.

The idea of this exercise is that you have everything you need to be happy, emotionally balanced, and confident. You simply need to call on your internal resources whenever it's required. As I mentioned above, some days it's hard to see yourself in a positive light. Your negative self-talk is loud, and your cons are happening in rapid succession.

In these moments, I want you to visualize the particular part of yourself you need. If you require more compassion, then call on your inner best

TABLE 7
Exercises to Build Optimism

Below is a list of activities that develop optimism. Practice these skills as you work through the book.

Skill	Activity	
Replace Cognition Errors	• Changing My Response • Prove It! • Recognizing the Cons	• Director's Notes • Shifting Thoughts • My Inner Experts
Mindset	• The Positive Side of Stress • How Stress Serves Me • Normalize My Fear • Prove It! • Jumps Toward Joy	• Thank You • What Do I Desire • Insane Courage • Dear Me • I Love Me
Empowering Statements	• I Choose • I've Got This • Prove It! • Director's Notes	• My Empowering Statements • My Inner Experts
Developing Optimism	• Insane Courage • Spot the Strength • Dear Me	• I Love Me • Shifting Thinking • Gratitude Reflection

friend, that part of you that is your personal cheerleader. If you need advice, then call on your inner voice of wisdom. If you are struggling to find courage, then call on your inner warrior. Whatever you need, learn to draw on the strength that exists inside, even when that trait feels elusive.

The development of optimism is an important aspect of your road to recovery. Practicing this skill will give you the perspective and flexibility you need to increase your self-compassion and improve your experience with life's setbacks, no matter how significant.

Gratitude and Joy

It seems only fitting that we end the book with a conversation about gratitude and joy. Researchers have confirmed something transformational psychologists and spiritual leaders have been saying for years: Expressions of gratitude, that feeling of thankfulness we sometimes experience, improve

MY INNER EXPERTS

Directions: Sometimes we need advice that we can't seem to find. When this happens, complete this chart. Indicate the problem and the type of expert you need. Then take a moment and pretend YOU are that expert. What advice would you give? Indicate that here.

Problem	What Kind of Expert Do I Need?	What Would That Expert Say About My Problem? What Advice Would He or She Give?

well-being. A grateful heart improves relationships and social connections. Acts of gratitude have consistently demonstrated a reduction in stress and anxiety and improved self-compassion (Petrocchi & Couyoumdjian, 2016). Pretty powerful, right?

I have long used gratitude practices both in my personal life and with my clients and the students I counsel. Few strategies have had as significant an impact for relatively little effort. The simple act of "counting your blessings" is enough to shift thinking, improve connections, and make you better at dealing with stress.

Many of the exercises you've completed increase your feelings of gratitude and joy (see Table 8 for a list of these). The Thank You letter and Jumps Toward Joy activities from Chapter 5 (see Activity 26 and Activity 25), in particular, cultivate a sense of thanksgiving and abundance.

Take a few moments and consider all of the ways you have begun to cultivate your feelings of gratitude and joy in this book. Which activities have impacted you the most? Are there other things, a gratitude or joy journal for example, that you'd like to try? As you think about your experiences with gratitude and joy, jot down your ideas on Activity 51: Gratitude Reflection. By taking stock of your current practices, you encourage yourself to grow even more.

Ashley's Story

Dear Ashley,

This is Mom. I know we've been through a lot of struggles together. The road through your anxiety, and mine, hasn't been easy. But I wanted to tell you a few things I've learned along the way.

You are an amazing young woman. Every day you face your inner demons, slaying them where they stand. You find something to feel good about, some way to push through the hardest of days. You are the strongest person I know.

You are kind and compassionate, despite how you feel inside. You share your light with the world, lend a helping hand to others, and continue to look for the best in people, no matter what you have going on in your own life.

TABLE 8
Exercises That Enhance Happiness and Joy

Below is a list of activities that enhance your joy through gratitude. Try the different activities any time you need a little push of joy of gratitude in your life.

Skill	Activity	
Mindset	♦ The Positive Side of Stress	♦ Thank You
	♦ How Stress Serves Me	♦ What Do I Desire
	♦ Normalize My Fear	♦ Insane Courage
	♦ Prove It!	♦ Dear Me
	♦ Jumps Toward Joy	♦ I Love Me
Gratitude	♦ Thank You	♦ Dear Me
	♦ Jumps Toward Joy	♦ Gratitude Reflection
	♦ Insane Courage	

You have many personal strengths and you are learning how to use them all. With each new skill, I watch your confidence and self-compassion grow. It often leaves me in awe.

As you continue to learn how to move past your stress and anxiety, I want you to know a few things—growth isn't linear. There will be many curves along the way, successes and failures. It is a messy journey. Embrace it! Be persistent and patient. Remember that you are strong and capable. Use your strengths. And remember that no matter what is going on, I am here.

I am your #1 fan, your cheerleader. I will carry the weight when you can't. I will remind you of all that you are and all that you will be. And I will loan you my strength or confidence any time you need it.

I love you,
Mom

This last chapter focused on positive psychology and the tools of gratitude, optimism, and happiness. These foundational skills increase resiliency overall. Taking time to evaluate and improve these areas will significantly increase your resiliency and improve your brain's integration, leading to greater coping capacity. Spend some time with the reflection questions listed below and your Road to Release action plan (Activity 33). Reflect on

ACTIVITY 51 ⇐
GRATITUDE REFLECTION

Directions: Take a moment to reflect on your journey through your anxiety and fear. What have you learned? What encouraged more joy, gratitude, compassion, and optimism? As you reflect on this journey, complete the chart below.

My Moments of Joy	*My Moments of Gratitude*
My Moments of Compassion	*My Moments of Optimism*

the progress you've made so far and what you'd like to accomplish in the future. The tools and strategies you've learned throughout the book were meant to serve you throughout your lifespan. Use them as frequently as you'd like.

Do the Work

Use these final questions to bring you to a deeper understanding of your thoughts and feelings about the information in this chapter. Consider focusing on one or two issues every time you journal.

- What am I grateful for in this moment? What brings me joy?
- What changes do I notice in my thinking after I've been focusing on gratitude for at least 3 weeks?
- I will take a moment to reflect on the journey I have taken. What changes do I notice in my life? In what ways has my experience with stress and anxiety changed?
- What risks am I more willing to take now as compared to before I read the book? What makes me more willing to step out of my comfort zone?
- What can I do right now to continue the work I've started through this book?

In addition to journaling, please take a moment to revisit the My Road to Release worksheet in Activity 33. Complete the third and fourth sections about your perspective and long-term goals. Setting and achieving goals can help solidify many of the new skills you've learned throughout the book.

FINAL THOUGHTS

The world can feel big and overwhelming at times. Sometimes, this sense of overload can result in significant feelings of stress and anxiety. And when this cycle repeats, we can find ourselves locked in the habit of negative thinking, overwhelming physical reactions, and spinning emotions. Although we can't control life's adventures or prevent the difficulties that sometimes come along for the ride, I hope that this book has provided some tools to help you break free from the paralyzing impact of extreme stress and anxiety. If these resources are not enough, reach out for support from your parents and a mental health professional.

From reframing your understanding of the role of stress in your life, to redefining your experiences with anxiety and panic, this book was developed to give you the information and tools required to help you balance your thoughts and emotions and build your resiliency. Every activity was included to assist you in your personal journey toward "letting go." It is my hope that through the process of reading and utilizing the strategies you have managed to forge a path through the muck and toward your own wellness.

Stress and anxiety need not prevent you from feeling connected to life. Furthermore, these emotional states need not dictate your life. Everyone experiences some levels of both stress and anxiety in their lives. The trick, I believe, is being able to move through the emotional upheaval without allowing the feelings to overwhelm your abilities to cope.

As you reread sections of the book and develop your Road to Release, I hope that you will share your successes, as well as the barriers you may encounter, with me either via e-mail (christine@chrsitinefonseca.com) or by joining in the conversation on Facebook at @IntenseLifeCoaching.

Before you leave, let me share one more idea with all of you—your personal experience with stress and anxiety is only one small piece of who you are as a human. It is not something that defines your whole self. As you travel through life and experience all of the ups and downs that may occur, remember that you are more than your stress or anxiety. At this moment, you are just as perfectly imperfect as you are meant to be. You will move past the limits of stress and anxiety. You will experience balance again.

All my best along this journey!

—*Christine Fonseca*

RECOMMENDED RESOURCES

Letting Go covers a variety of topics within the field of stress, anxiety, and panic. Any of the individual sections and chapters could have been its own book. What I've covered represents a basic understanding of stress, anxiety, and how to move from dysfunctional to functional responses to these behaviors. The recommended readings below provide additional sources of information regarding not only stress management, anxiety, and panic, but also many of the positive psychology skills referenced.

Stress, Anxiety, and Panic

The following books offer some of my favorite strategies and interventions to provide you with a deeper understanding of your anxiety and assist you along your Road to Release:

- *The Road to Calm Workbook: Life-Changing Tools to Stop Runaway Emotions* by Carolyn Daitch and Lissah Lorberbaum

- *The Stress Reduction Workbook for Teens: Mindfulness Skills to Help You Deal With Stress* by Gina M. Biegel
- *The Anxiety Workbook for Teens: Activities to Help You Deal With Anxiety and Worry* by Lisa M. Schab
- *When Panic Attacks: The New Drug-Free Anxiety Therapy That Can Change Your Life* by David D. Burns
- *The Anxiety Survival Guide for Teens: CBT Skills to Overcome Fear, Worry, and Panic* by Jennifer Shannon
- *My Anxious Mind: A Teen's Guide to Managing Anxiety and Panic* by Michael A. Tompkins and Katherine Martinez

Happiness and Kindness

The cultivation of happiness, self-compassion, and kindness are fundamental skills within the field of positive psychology. The following books offer additional insight into the development of a happiness mindset:
- *Search Inside Yourself: The Unexpected Path to Achieving Success, Happiness (and World Peace)* by Chade-Meng Tan
- *The How of Happiness: A New Approach to Getting the Life You Want* by Sonja Lyubomirsky
- *The Happiness Project: Or Why I Spent A Year Trying to Sing in the Morning, Clean My Closets, Fight Right, Read Aristotle, and Generally Have More Fun* by Gretchen Rubin
- *Real Happiness: The Power of Meditation* by Sharon Salzberg
- *Kindness Boomerang: How to Save the World (and Yourself) Through 365 Daily Acts* by Orly Wahba

Mindfulness

Throughout the book, I mentioned mindfulness and present moment awareness. The following books offer a deeper understanding of mindfulness, as well as great strategies for mastering this tool:
- *The Mindful Teen: Powerful Skills to Help You Handle Stress One Moment at a Time* by Dzung X. Vo
- *Learning to Breathe: A Mindfulness Curriculum for Adolescents to Cultivate Emotion Regulation, Attention, and Performance* by Patricia C. Broderick

- *Mindfulness: An Eight-Week Plan for Finding Peace in a Frantic World* by Mark Williams and Danny Penman

Empowerment and Inspiration

Sometimes you just need a little inspiration and guidance. The following books are filled with advice, strategies, and stories that inspire:
- *There's a Hole in My Sidewalk: The Romance of Self-Discovery* by Portia Nelson
- *The Girls' Book of Wisdom: Empowering, Inspirational Quotes From Over 400 Fabulous Females* edited by Catherine Dee
- *Chocolate for a Teen's Soul: Life-Changing Stories for Young Women About Growing Wise and Growing Strong* by Kay Allenbaugh
- *Staying Strong* by Demi Lovato

Finally, I wanted to share a couple of my favorite inspirational stories of girls facing life with courage and strength:
- *I Am Malala: How One Girl Stood Up for Education and Changed the World* (Young Readers Edition) by Malala Yousafzai
- *Being Jazz: My Life as a (Transgender) Teen* by Jazz Jennings
- *The Butterfly Mosque: A Young American Woman's Journey to Love and Islam* by G. Willow Wilson

REFERENCES

American Psychological Association. (n.d.). *Understanding chronic stress.* Retrieved from http://www.apa.org/help center/understanding-chronic-stress.aspx

American Psychological Association. (2017). *Stress in America 2017 snapshot: Coping with change.* Retrieved from http://www.apa.org/news/press/releases/stress/2016/coping-with-change.pdf

Bamber, M. D., & Schneider, J. K. (2016). Mindfulness-based meditation to decrease stress and anxiety in college students: A narrative synthesis of the research. *Educational Research Review, 18,* 1–32.

Biegel, G. M. (2009). *The stress reduction workbook for teens: Mindfulness skills to help you deal with stress.* Oakland, CA: Instant Help Books.

Bourne, E. J. (2015). *The anxiety and phobia workbook* (6th ed.). Oakland, CA: New Harbinger.

Burns, D. D. (2006). *When panic attacks: The new drug-free anxiety therapy that can change your life.* New York, NY: Harmony Books.

Crowe, C. (Director). (2011). *We bought a zoo* [Motion Picture]. United States: 20th Century Fox.

Crum, A., & Phillips, D. J. (2015). Self-fulfilling prophesies, placebo effects, and the social-psychological creation of reality. *Emerging Trends in the Social and Behavioral Sciences: An Interdisciplinary, Searchable, and Linkable Resource, 1–14.*

Csikszentmihalyi, M. (2008). *Flow: The psychology of optimal experience.* New York, NY: Harper.

Daitch, C., & Lorberbaum, L. (2016). *The road to calm workbook: Life-changing tools to stop runaway emotions.* New York, NY: Norton.

Duan, W., & Bu, H. (2017). Randomized trial investigating of a single-session character-strength-based cognitive intervention on freshman's adaptability. *Research on Social Work Practice, 23,* 336–345. doi:10.1177/1049731517699525

Fonseca, C. (2011). *101 success secrets for gifted kids: The ultimate handbook.* Waco, TX: Prufrock Press.

Fonseca, C. (2013). *The girl guide: Finding your place in a mixed-up world.* Waco, TX: Prufrock Press.

Fonseca, C. (2015). *Raising the shy child: A parent's guide to social anxiety.* Waco, TX: Prufrock Press.

Fonseca, C. (2016). *Emotional intensity in gifted students: Helping kids cope with explosive feelings* (2nd ed.). Waco, TX: Prufrock Press.

Hill, P. L., & Turiano, N. A. (2014). Purpose in life as a predictor of mortality across adulthood. *Psychological Science, 25,* 1482–1486.

Kendall, P. C., & Peterman, J. S. (2017). CBT for adolescents with anxiety: Mature yet still developing. *Focus, 15,* 227–239.

Kranzler, A., Young, J. F., Hankin, B. L., Abela, J. R., Elias, M. J., & Selby, E. A. (2016). Emotional awareness: A transdiagnostic predictor of depression and anxiety for children and adolescents. *Journal of Clinical Child & Adolescent Psychology, 45,* 262–269. doi:10.1080/15374416.2014.987379

Liu, R. T. (2013). Stress generation: Future directions and clinical implications. *Clinical Psychology Review, 33,* 406–416.

Mancini, A. D., Littleton, H. L., & Grills, A. E. (2016). Can people benefit from acute stress? Social support, psychological improvement, and resilience after the Virginia Tech campus shootings. *Clinical Psychological Science, 4,* 401–417.

McGonigal, K. (2015). *The upside of stress: Why stress is good for you, and how to get good at it.* New York, NY: Avery.

Mee, B. (2008). *We bought a zoo: The amazing true story of a young family, a broken down zoo, and the 200 wild animals that changed their lives forever.* New York, NY: Weinstein Books.

Mongrain, M., & Anselmo-Matthews, T. (2012). Do positive psychology exercises work? A replication of Seligman et al. *Journal of Clinical Psychology, 68,* 382–389.

Morimoto, Y., Takahashi, M., & Namiki, K. (2015). Using a character strengths program to increase self-formation consciousness of high school girls. *Japanese Journal of Educational Psychology, 63,* 181–191. http://dx.doi.org/10.5926/jjep.63.181

Neff, K., & Davidson, O. (2016). Self-compassion: Embracing suffering with kindness. In I. Ivtzan & T. Lomas (Eds.), *Mindfulness in positive psychology: The science of meditation and wellbeing* (pp. 37–50). Abingdon, England: Routledge.

Nelson, P. (2002). *There's a hole in my sidewalk: The romance of self-discovery* (35th anniversary ed.). New York, NY: Atria Books.

Parks, A. C., & Layous, K. (2016). Positive psychology interventions. In A. M. Wood & J. Johnson (Eds.), *The Wiley handbook of positive clinical psychology* (pp. 305–320). West Sussex, England: Wiley. doi:10.1002/9781118468197.ch21

Paruthi, S., Brooks, L. J., D'Ambrosio, C., Hall, W. A., Kotagal, S., Lloyd, R. M., . . . & Rosen, C. L. (2016). Recommended amount of sleep for pediatric populations: A consensus statement of the American Academy of Sleep Medicine. *Journal of Clinical Sleep Medicine, 12,* 785.

Petrocchi, N., & Couyoumdjian, A. (2016). The impact of gratitude on depression and anxiety: The mediating role of criticizing, attacking and reassuring the self. *Self and Identity, 15,* 191–205.

Powers, M. B., Asmundson, G. J. G., & Smits, J. A. J. (2015). Exercise for mood and anxiety disorders: The state-of-the science. *Cognitive Behaviour Therapy, 44,* 237–239. http://doi.org/10.1080/16506073.2015.1047286

Robinson, B. A. (2009). *Religious society of friends (Quakers): Beliefs and practices.* Retrieved from http://www.religioustolerance.org/quaker2.htm

Seligman, M. (2011). *Learned optimism: How to change your mind and your life.* New York, NY: Vintage.

Shaddix, J., Esperance, T., & Churko, K. (Composers). (2014). *Face everything and rise* [Recorded by Papa Roach]. On *F.E.A.R* [CD]. Los Angeles, CA: Eleven Seven Music.

Stress management. (n.d.). Retrieved from http://www.timethoughts.com/stress/stress-management.htm

Tarokh, L., Saletin, J. M., & Carskadon, M. A. (2016). Sleep in adolescence: Physiology, cognition and mental health. *Neuroscience & Biobehavioral Reviews, 70*, 182–188.

Unger, C. A., Busse, D., & Yim, I. S. (2017). The effect of guided relaxation on cortisol and affect: Stress reactivity as a moderator. *Journal of Health Psychology, 22*, 29–38.

Weekes, C. (1990). *Peace from nervous suffering.* New York, NY: Signet.

Zucker, B. (2017). *Anxiety-free kids: An interactive guide for parents and children* (2nd ed.). Waco, TX: Prufrock Press.

Zwick, E. (Director). (2003). *The last samurai* [Motion Picture]. United States: Warner Bros.

ABOUT THE AUTHOR

Trained as a school psychologist, **Christine Fonseca** is dedicated to helping children and adults explore and connect with their personal truth. She is an award-winning author of both nonfiction and fiction; a nationally recognized speaker on topics related to educational psychology, giftedness, and soulful writing; and an international consultant and coach. Christine has written self-help articles for Parents.com, Johnson & Johnson, *Bop/Tiger Beat*, and *Justine Magazine*. Her award-winning titles include *Emotional Intensity in Gifted Students: Helping Kids Cope With Explosive Feelings*, *Raising the Shy Child: A Parent's Guide to Social Anxiety Disorder*, and *I'm Not Just Gifted: Social-Emotional Curriculum for Guiding Gifted Children*.

When she isn't traveling or lost in a new storyline, Christine can be found sitting on a beach with a book in hand, drinking too many skinny lattes in the local coffee house, or exploring the world with her family. For more information about Christine Fonseca, or to find out more about her books, coaching services, and online courses, visit her website at http://christinefonseca.com.